THE DAY WE WENT TO ARSENAL

Carlisle United and the 1951 FA Cup

THE DAY WE WENT TO ARSENAL

Carlisle United and the 1951 FA Cup

Martin Daley

First published 2014 by DB Publishing, an imprint of JMD Media Ltd, Nottingham, United Kingdom.

ISBN 9781780913674

Printed and bound by Copytech (UK) Limited, Peterborough.

Contents

For 12-year-old Paul Daley and his dad Claude

Introduction

At about twenty past five on Wednesday 20 June 2012, I found myself standing on the corner of Finkle Street and Fisher Street in Carlisle. I was one of an estimated 30,000 people in and around the Bitts Park area of the city waiting for the Olympic Torch relay to pass by. It was an event that caught the imagination of the whole city, along with the rest of the country. As someone said on national radio, "Go along, it's great – I don't know why, *it just is!*" And he was right – as the torch passed by, everyone instinctively broke ranks and followed it, Pied Piper fashion, to its destination in the park where activities and a concert rounded off the celebrations for everyone in attendance.

It was a classic example of where an event can transcend its sporting (or sports-related) roots. The torch relay, and the Olympics (and Paralympics) completely captured the imagination of the whole country and gave us all a collective feelgood factor rarely experienced. It seemed that all we watched, read and talked about for two months solid was Olympics-related.

We all cheered on, and loved our sporting heroes who appeared to love representing us, which meant we loved them all the more. Non-sports fans too were engrossed by London 2012. And even avid *football* fans seemed to enjoy the diversion from the present day gaudy rapaciousness of English football, with its outrageous ticket prices, its astronomical player salaries, and its shadowy foreign owners, half of whom appear to have achieved their vast wealth through dubious means. Today, the separation of football clubs and its players, from the people who pay to watch them (the fans) is complete. It has ceased to be 'the people's game' it once was.

The only reason the Olympic Torch Relay won't merit great mention in the twenty-first century chapter of Carlisle's history is because virtually every town and village around the country experienced the same event.

Over sixty years earlier however, something similar happened – but this time it was unique to Carlisle. Thousands of people lined the same streets we did over sixty years later, to be involved in a sporting event that provided them with a brief respite from their austere, mundane lives, and allowed them to believe that great things were possible for the underdog.

The year was 1951.

King George VI was still on the throne, whilst his Prime Minister was Clement Attlee (although Winston Churchill would defeat him in the October General Election). The country was still on rationing as it recovered from a World War, and many of its servicemen were off fighting a different war in Korea. Anglo-Egyptian relations soured, threatening to destabilise the Middle East [leading to the Suez Crisis five years later] and as the Cold War started to get decidedly nippy, Guy Burgess and Donald MacLean defected to the USSR.

In the world of art and entertainment giants of the literary world Christie, Greene and Lewis all saw publications that year. While on radio (there was little or no television for the masses) *The Archers* and *The Goon Show* were broadcast for the first time.

In the world of sport, the great baseball player Joe DiMaggio played his final game, while Glasgow-born Bobby Thompson hit the most famous home run of all time – 'the shot that was heard round the world.' Juan Manuel Fangio won his first Formula One World Championship and Randolph Turpin beat the great Sugar Ray Robinson to become Middleweight Champion of the World.

All of these historic happenings overshadow an event that involved the city of Carlisle when 1951 was barely a week old. The event in question was Carlisle United's third round FA Cup tie. *A mere football match?* some sniffy historians might ask. Well, it might have started out as two football teams being drawn out of a hat to play each other in the cup, but it quickly snowballed into something much bigger. Not only did it become the biggest game in the club's (then) 47-year history, as the opponents were the mighty Arsenal from *that there London*, it became a significant chapter in Carlisle's post-war social history.

Make no mistake, if Carlisle United drew Arsenal in the cup today it would be a big deal: Carlisle are a small, reasonably well-run provincial club while Arsenal are one of the top teams in the country (as these words are written they sit on top of both the Premier League and have just qualified for the latter stages of the Champions' League). But in 1951 the positions of the two clubs were exaggerated several fold.

Carlisle United were virtually unheard of; their only real claim to fame was that Sunderland inside-forward (and soon to be England International) Ivor Broadis had started his post-war career there. The club plied its trade in the lower half of the Third Division North (the third tier was the lowest league in the country and was split into North and South to save clubs unnecessary travelling costs).

Arsenal, on the other hand, were the biggest and best club in the country (it would be the late 1950s and into the 1960s before Manchester United and later Liverpool would wrestle such a status away). They boasted a team full of internationals and had won the First Division title in 1948; they were also the FA Cup holders, having won the trophy in 1950. In short, to say this was a David and Goliath encounter is an understatement.

But it is said that the bigger they are the harder they fall, and the sling that was designed to bring the blue-bloods crashing down was swung by Carlisle's charismatic rookie manager – a young Scot called Bill Shankly. Shankly's unswerving self-belief rubbed off on his players and the whole city as they prepared for the mammoth task. "I'm a people's man," Shankly would say later in his career, "only the people matter." Throughout his professional life, the people responded to this ethos and grew to idolise him for it.

The event (because that's what it was – an event, not just a football match) was the first major post-war event Carlisle had seen. It completely captured the imagination of the whole city; everyone wanted to be part of the adventure that would break the austere existence of ration-ruled Britain. Several chartered trains carried fans down to London for the game and when their team incredibly got a draw, the scramble for replay-tickets became legendary.

One young lad who was lucky enough to see both games was 12-year-old Paul Daley, who went to down to London and then to Brunton Park with his dad Claude.

I must have been around the same age as Paul when I first became aware of the adventure. For some reason, when I was even younger, I latched on to Arsenal and they became 'my team' – I've followed them ever since. When I became aware that my dad had witnessed this historic meeting between Carlisle and Arsenal all those years ago, I couldn't get enough of the story: he must have told me about it a hundred times; I must have asked him about it a hundred more.

When I entered adulthood and could afford to do a little travelling about myself, I would watch Arsenal play their away games in the north of England and go down to London to see them at their ground – Highbury – two or three times a season. Some years ago we were all going on a family weekend to London and I managed to get some tickets for a home game against Leeds United. Paul Daley has therefore been to Highbury twice in his life: once with his dad in 1951 and once with his son, forty-five years later.

I had often flirted with the idea of writing something about the '51 adventure because of my love for Arsenal and Carlisle, but when I discovered, in the library a treasure trove of photographs of the games, the players returning home, and the queue for tickets, I knew I just had to do it.

I finished writing this book on Sunday 15 December 2013. It was the day of Nelson Mandela's funeral. As I watched that event on television, I was reminded of one of his famous speeches when he spoke about how sport can change the world; how it has the power to inspire, and how it can unite people in a way that nothing else can. This is what the Olympics did for us in 2012, and 'the Arsenal game' did the same thing for the people of Carlisle all those years ago.

To fully understand how the people got so carried away, we must first consider the lives they led. The book therefore starts during the war, where we first meet some of the people who were to experience the adventure.

Learning about their homes, their work, and the general austerity, helps us to understand why this was such a big deal; and how the event acted as a few weeks of escapism from their tough existence. The book therefore is part social history as well as a sporting one.

The story is peppered with coincidence, irony and comedy as the characters and protagonists involved, and the spectators who watched them continually cross each other's path; a path that will lead them all to the same place on 6 January 1951.

Martin Daley
Carlisle
2013

Acknowledgements

The obvious thanks must go to the people who were involved in the adventure in one way or another. Whether they be a supporter, a player, a family member, or just someone who remembered the whole event, this book would have not been possible without them. So here goes, thanks to:

Pat Baty and her dad Nick, Jim 'Jazza' Boyle, Ivor Broadis, Stuart Brown, Willie Cannon, Ellen Carruthers and her son Mike, Paul Daley, Maggie Economopoulos, Leigh Edwards, Bob Forbes, Gerald Irwin, Ronnie Jones, Sam Kirk, Gordon Lawson, John Lindsay, Harry Notman, Eric Thompson and Doreen Waters.

Thanks also to Carlisle United historian David Steele in allowing me to access his player interviews and checking the facts in this book. His help and courtesy was matched by Harry's son, John Notman, whose collection of United memorabilia is staggering.

As usual, I owe a debt of gratitude to Stephen White and his colleagues at Carlisle Library for their help, support and use of facilities. Similarly, Stewart Blair, Photo Editor at the *Cumberland News*, was equally supportive and obliging when searching for, and allowing me to use some of the images from the archives. Thanks also to Ashley Kendall for allowing me to use some photographs from his wonderful local collection; and also Elizabeth Nelson and Carlisle City Council. Every effort has been made in contacting copyright-holders of other images – I believe they are: Arsenal Football Club, Chris Wright, Getty images, *The Daily Mail, The Guardian*. If I have missed crediting anyone else, I apologise.

As ever, I should also mention my proof-reading pal Christophe Vever who never lets me down, thanks mate – *beaudy!*

Last but not least, thanks to Steve and the team at DB Publishing for once again supporting me and allowing me to write the books I want to write.

Thanks again to everyone concerned.

It's Grim Up North

In all honesty, it was grim everywhere. To suggest that the people of Britain waved the 1940s goodbye with a begrudging 'good riddance' is an understatement. They had lived through the hell of a world war that dominated the decade, and the legacy of which was still having an effect as the 1950s approached.

Winston Churchill may have led the country to victory during the war but the General Election of 1945 provided a resounding assertion that the country didn't want him as their peacetime leader. The previous generation had suffered mass unemployment and homelessness following *their* world war, the working classes of the 1940s were not prepared to suffer the same fate. The Labour Party, under Clement Atlee promised social reform and the people of Britain responded by giving them a mandate in the form of a staggering landslide victory.

Once in power, Labour took 20 per cent of the national wealth into public ownership and called it 'nationalisation'. The premise was that public ownership of railways, steelworks and mines would result in a fairer distribution of the country's wealth that hitherto had been monopolised by rich, southern England. With the commitment to building publicly owned, rented council housing, and the creation of the National Health Service in 1948, the downtrodden populace could look forward to a brighter future. That was the theory anyway.

As these words are written in the second decade of the twenty-first century, and the country works its way through a recession, Central Government are keen to have us believe that 'we are all in this together.'

But in our cosmopolitan age, there appears to be little sense of belonging, and even less of a sense of looking out for one's neighbour. The gap between the haves and the have-nots seems to widen year-on-year, and the aforementioned lame comment only serves to weaken ordinary people's faith in officialdom.

Our parents and grandparents were brought up in an era where families had been ravaged and broken by the war; the wider community therefore served as the family. Paul Daley lived through the hardship as a child and says today, "We really were all in it together then. Everyone really was in the same boat – nobody had anything!" In order to fully understand the context of Paul's comment, we have to go back a further generation.

His father Claude Daley was born in Carlisle in 1910. In adulthood he married Nora Scott and worked for William Blaylock Anderson, the fruit merchant on West Walls, who had been operating in the city since 1898.

Like so many Carlisle firms of the period, W.B. Anderson had a paternalistic approach to his customers and his employees. One of Claude's colleagues at Anderson's in the late 1930s was delivery driver Bert Graham. It's clear listening to Bert, the affection shown by his employer towards his staff was reciprocated:

> W.B Anderson was a great man, a great business man. He cared a lot for his staff and he was a good worker, regularly being down at the station at 4 o'clock in the morning with the workers to help unload the trains.

Claude would be there too, supervising the unloading of fruit and vegetables for the Carlisle warehouse, and then organising the appropriate distribution to the other Anderson branches at Windermere and Glasgow.

From the station, it would then be back to his role as warehouse manager on West Walls, where he assumed responsibilities for everything in the building, from organising deliveries to tending to the exotic fruits in the ripening room.

Bert meanwhile would load up his vehicle and set out east of Carlisle, delivering to Brampton, Haltwhistle and Alston. If there was a particularly heavy load, Claude would double up as delivery assistant.

W.B. Anderson's warehouse on West Walls in the 1920s

The sense of 'family' demonstrated at Anderson's was typical of the companies of the day. Carlisle was a working class town and it seems the firms were aware of their responsibilities, when it came to their workers. If the West Walls' fruit merchant was one of the more modest, in terms of numbers, then one of the biggest employers was Carr's Biscuit Works in Caldewgate.

The firm was started by Jonathan Dodson Carr in 1831. Carr was a Quaker and his Christian values were prominent from a very early stage when he established a schoolroom for the children of his workers, and a library and reading room for children and adults alike.

Carr genuinely cared about his fellow-man: looking after his workers, actively fighting *against* the slave trade, and *for* the temperance movement. Carr also recognised the need for economic and social reform and involved himself in the establishment of gas and water supplies in the city, as well as the founding of the Cumberland Building Society.

Carr's descendants continued the founder's altruism towards the company's employees; a century after its founding, the factory was probably the second largest employer (behind the railways) in the city.

Jonathan Carr's fellow businessman and Quaker, Hudson Scott, complemented the biscuit production by manufacturing tin boxes for them to be packed it. Scott and sons were another to start their business in the mid-nineteenth century and by the 1930s the large factory on James Street was another jewel in the crown of the industrial city.

The two complemented each other perfectly, with Scott's tins turning Carr's biscuits into a global brand (not that anyone knew what a 'global brand' was in 1930).

Hudson Scott, like Carr and others, prided themselves on enriching the lot of their workers: working hours were reasonable (for the period), while health, wellbeing and camaraderie were encouraged through sports and social activities. This in turn all contributed to a feeling of pride in the employee's organisation, as father followed son into *their* firm.

The third colossus (in every sense) that put Carlisle on the world's industrial map was the crane maker, Cowans and Sheldon.

Like it's two city 'cousins', the firm was another nineteenth century establishment – the brainchild of North-Easterners John Cowans, Edward Sheldon and brothers, William and Thomas Bouch.

By the second decade of the twentieth century the company had become Britain's best known crane maker; such was their reputation for excellence, orders were received from all around the globe for their cranes and hardware.

Part of the massive Cowans and Sheldon yard at St Nicholas, Carlisle

At a reunion of Cowans's workers in the twenty-first century, Joe Hope spoke of typical fondness for his employer:

> I worked there for 37 years and became commissioning engineer and safety officer by the time of my retirement. My dad worked there for 50 years before me and even my mum worked there during the First World War. Lots of families worked side by side, that's what made it what it was.

Fred McMurray was another young man who walked into the enormous Cowans's yard at St Nicholas, Carlisle. He was 13 years old in 1939 and the need for such youngsters would increase later that year as events elsewhere were about to shape the destiny of the workers from Carr's, Hudson Scott's, Cowans – and W.B. Anderson.

One of Anderson's sons, John, had only joined his father's company in 1937. He was working in the Glasgow office at the time and volunteered to join the territorials when war broke out.

Another volunteer was his father's warehouseman in Carlisle. At the commencement of the war Claude lived with his wife Nora and son Paul on Greta Avenue. In September 1939 – before conscription, and much to his wife's displeasure – Claude joined the Royal Engineers as a driver. Within a month, his rank was changed to Sapper and he shipped to France on operations in the spring of 1940.

By June he was captured by the Germans and sent to Stalag XXA in German occupied Poland, where he was to remain as a Prisoner Of War for the majority of the war.

Back home, the dreaded 'Reported missing' correspondence was received on the 24 June before a month later, a further correspondence was received informing his wife that he had been taken as a POW.

During Claude's internment, he managed to send and receive the odd correspondence and his caring employer Anderson's would often send him food parcels (another example of the employer's concern and sense of responsibility).

Home-life for the wife and son he left behind was mirrored by millions of others – this particular fatherless wartime family staying with Nora's parents in Milton Street, Caldewgate. Nora fought her own battle with silent pneumonia during the war, which put an even greater emphasis on the wider family unit: grandparents, aunties – and when *they* were not around – friends and neighbours.

The war was only four months old when food rationing was introduced throughout the country. Limits were imposed on the sale of bacon, butter and sugar; two months later, meat became rationed, and it would not be long before clothing coupons were introduced.

With children sleeping in the same beds as adults, communal outside washing and toilet facilities, women doing men's work in the factories while they were away fighting, and queues outside shops (while those inside bartered for extra food), it's difficult to imagine such hardship for those of us who haven't lived through it.

What we have today it seems, is the glamourised, almost sanitised version of the past viewed by many through rose-coloured glasses. I conclude that people who bang on about 'the good old days!' probably never had the misfortune of living through them.

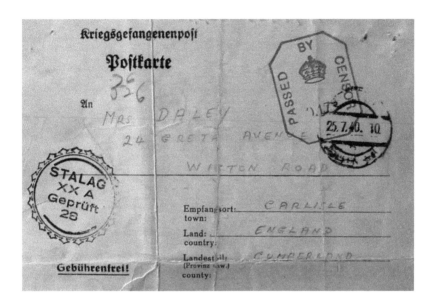

Notification of Claude being taken Prisoner of War in July 1940

Sapper Daley (seated left) with some of his fellow POWs at Stalag XXA c1943

For example, we all seemed to have grown up with the endearing (almost romantic) images of what it must have been like to escape from a Second World War German prison camp. Every Christmas Day afternoon we sit in front of the telly watching Steve McQueen tearing round the Bavarian countryside on his stolen motorcycle in his snazzy leather jacket.

Reality of course was very different; the prisoners were determined to make their escape whichever way they could. Whether through a painstakingly planned attempt, or just shear opportunism and bravado, these men were prepared to take a chance and risk it all to break from their captors.

Sapper Claude Daley later gave an insight to the general feelings of the POWs when he once told his grandson, "We didn't care; when we saw or heard our planes overhead we would run out onto the parade ground and cheer them on." When he and his colleagues then saw a chance to leg it, they promptly did so. Stalag XXA was not a stereotypical Colditz-type castle; it was a series of forts and satellite work camps south of Gdansk that stood by the *Vistula* River.

After two unsuccessful break-out attempts in his five years of captivity (something for which the guards would give all would-be escapees, "a good hiding") he was finally successful in evading his captors in the final months of the war. Little did he know that he was jumping out of the frying pan and into the fire.

By 1945, Hitler's dreams were crumbling. He ordered all of his prison camps in the east to close and instructed his generals to march the POWs west to Berlin. Meanwhile, that other lunatic, Stalin, was steamrollering his way across Eastern Europe. Twenty thousand people were losing their lives each day as the two tyrants ensured the region went into political, military and social meltdown.

Sapper Daley and his six hundred fellow-POWs received the order on 21 January 1945 to vacate Stalag XXA. One poor soul later described the hardship that followed:

> My comrades and I marched 20–40 km per day through two–three feet of snow and 25 degrees of frost. I had to sleep three nights out

in open fields in such conditions. In 21 days we never received a hot meal. Sick men were forced to carry on for 21 days without attention.

It was during this march that Claude and several colleagues slipped away from their increasingly disorganised captors. After sleeping for a night in a barn on the Polish/German border, they were picked up by the advancing Russians. It should be stressed that they were supposed to be allies but it was their conviction that the British soldiers were, in fact, deserting Germans. Cue their first beating.

Claude later recalled that at one point, he and his colleagues were about to be shot by firing squad, when a Red Cross official established they were British and convinced their captors of the fact. "Five weeks with the Russians was worse than five years with the Germans," Claude later concluded.

It could be said that the Daleys of Caldewgate were at the other end of the social spectrum to those of the Carr dynasty, despite the fact that Carr's Biscuit Works was only a couple of hundred yards from their Milton Street home. But this was a day and age where everyone really *was* all in it together, and the war made no allowance for class or status. The two families shared years of worry, as another Carlisle POW was a member of that Carr dynasty. Captain Richard Carr would be awarded an MBE for *his* repeated escape attempts from various prison camps during the war.

Back home meanwhile, Richard's family firm were doing their bit for the war effort. It wasn't just in parishes where companies of Home Guard were formed: large works formed their own, consisting of male workers who were exempt from military service (on the grounds of age, disability etc). Carr's Biscuits had one such company. And Richard's family members were also mucking in – his cousin Margaret Carr was working in the family factory while he was incarcerated.

History was not only repeating itself for the men of Britain, whose fathers had gone away to war a generation earlier; it was also repeating itself for the women of the country who had to take up their husbands' roles in factories and warehouses across the country.

Cowans and Sheldon was a typical example where it was not only youngsters like Fred McMurray who found themselves working there before school-leaving age; another war time Cowans employee was Bell Curran.

She worked as a welder in the giant yard while her husband Neil was serving in India with the Royal Armoured Corps. Such was the lot of the matriarch figure of the early 1940s: holding down a job and doing their bit for the war effort, whilst at the same time looking after children at home.

Bell Curran, welder at Cowans and Sheldon c1943

In Bell's case, she had a son, Billy, and a daughter Noeline, who was born in 1940 and therefore never knew her dad until he came home after being injured in India in 1944. The young child didn't know any other life than the fatherless one she had been born into; hers was another household full of grandparents and aunties. "I didn't like the look of him when he first came back," recalls Noeline today, "I couldn't take to him at all."

The Currans lived off Upperby Road in Carlisle. Their readjustment to peacetime life was mirrored all over the country as soldiers were demobbed and returned home to 'normality', whatever that was.

Across in Caldewgate, Nora Daley woke her son Paul (aged seven) one night in October 1945, to introduce him to *his* dad Claude, who had managed to escape the shackles of both the Germans and the Russians. (Paul remembers his dad being in uniform, with his kit bag and rifle.)

It was a typical scene played out in tens of thousands of households across the country as returning servicemen tried to re-integrate themselves into society and family life. Not an easy task when their own children didn't even know them.

If such stories are poignant to us today, others are unimaginable. Jim Boyle – known affectionately throughout his subsequent seventy years to many in Carlisle as 'Jazza' – was representative of greater heartache. His dad was killed while serving in the embryonic SAS in 1943:

> There was just me and my mother. We lived in digs in and around the city: aunties, uncles, and rented accommodation, anywhere to keep a roof over our heads I suppose. My mother took cleaning and cooking jobs to keep us going.

For those who *did* return, and were fortunate enough to have a job, it was back to work. Claude Daley returned to his job as warehouseman at W.B. Anderson's. There was no post-traumatic stress disorder, no prisoner of war syndrome, and no compensation either; just the unknown, unseen wounds of war. Like the vast majority of his peers, Claude carried his burden with a silent dignity.

In his absence Anderson's had suspended their fruit and veg' distribution and taken on the responsibility for the distribution of cooking fat, margarine, lard and other rations instead. Now the business set about re-establishing itself amid the uncertainty of post-war Britain.

Peace and 'victory' may well have been achieved, but could the pre-war 'stability' enjoyed by the Carlisle workforce ever be re-established? The city certainly didn't have the bomb scars as some others, but with a changing workforce and an uncertainty about the post-war market, and rationing here for the foreseeable future, there seemed very little to be optimistic about.

And what optimism there was for the city's industry was dented as early as the 31 October 1945 when Hudson Scott & Sons Ltd was liquidated and was merged with Metal Box, the parent company who had acquired a controlling interest of the Carlisle firm in 1921. Local management were determined to keep their local identify and succeeded in achieving permission from the parent company to retain the name of the great man.

It was against this uncertain backdrop that the 1945 General Election was fought.Churchill based his campaign on three main assumptions: first, that the obligations of gratitude of the people would return him to power; secondly, Britain would lose its identify under a socialist government; and thirdly, that the nation's continued existence under Conservative leadership would predicate the survival and continuity of the Empire.

To his utter astonishment (and that of many contemporary commentators), he was proved wrong on all three fronts.

History would judge Winston Churchill as arguably the greatest Briton of all time for his stoicism and leadership during the war, but like all great leaders he polarized opinion. Bell Curran, like many of her generation had a straight-between-the-eyes directness about her, "He was just an old tosspot!" was her considered opinion in later life.

A bit harsh you might say? But the view was shared by many of the working classes who were not prepared to suffer the mass unemployment and hardship their parents had experienced after *their* World War.

Instead they elected Clement Atlee's Labour Party into government with a landslide victory (Labour returned 393 to the Conservatives' 213). But by the mid-way point of their administration, the nationalisation programme and the introduction of the Health Service were not delivering the promises quickly enough for the people of Britain. And when the brutal winters of 1947 and 1948 crippled the food supply, and taking the fuel shortages into consideration, it meant there was unlikely to be an end to the rationing programme any time soon.

Social housing remained a major problem and those that were lucky enough to have their own home were hardly living in the lap of luxury.

Sam Kirk was a young man living with his parents at Longsowerby, Carlisle following the war. Having left school at 14 in 1940, two years later he found employment on the railway, the city's biggest employer. Starting as a cleaner and graduating to a position of fireman (earning £3, 6s per week), he remembers conditions at home:

> My mother used to use a scrubbing brush and washboard in the bath to do the washing. I worked as fireman on the railway so you can imagine what my shirts were like! The only heating we had was the coal fire. Women used to shop every day because there were no fridges. They were hard times.

Amusement was in short supply for the populace. Home entertainment consisted of listening to the wireless (or as the BBC presenters would pronounce it – *whaarless*) – a large wooden box with two or three knobs on that took up a corner of the living room.

The wireless was a key component in the home in post war Britain, especially for women and children. People may well have pulled together during the traumatic decade but it was still an era before gender and age equality, and everyone knew their place as a result.

When kids weren't making their own fun outside, playing marbles or kicking a tatty old tennis ball around the dusty streets, (*yes, kids played outside in those days!*) they were listening to *Dick Barton Special Agent* or *The Younger Generation*.

Mothers meanwhile were treated to *Women's Hour, Housewives' Choice* and *Mrs Dale's Diary*

The wireless also provided one of the few opportunities for the family to come together as a unit to listen to quiz shows and *Family Favourites*.

The other escape for the masses came through the picture houses. Children's imagination would be fired by the minors on a Saturday morning, while their parents would lose themselves alongside the likes of Spencer Tracy or Elizabeth Taylor in the evening, at the dozen or so cinemas that were dotted around the city.

(At the start of the war, the Government shut down all cinemas and radio channels apart from the Home Service. People were so demoralised however that picture houses were re-opened and the *Light Programme* – light entertainment – was reintroduced on the wireless. At the end of the war the *Third Programme* – which seemed to focus mainly on classical music – was introduced.)

Another post war radio show that proved popular with listeners was *Down Your Way*, presented by the broadcasting giant of the day Richard Dimbleby. The premise of the programme was to broadcast from a different town or city each week, giving the listener a feeling for what life was like in that particular part of the country. (*As harsh as it was for themselves probably!*)

In 1949 the programme came to Carlisle and inevitably visited the Carr's Biscuit Works.

Richard Dimbleby (left) and producer John Shuter of Down Your Way interview Lilian Small at Carr's in 1949

The employers of the city were doing their best to re-ignite the 'family' spirit amongst their workers by organising dances and social gatherings, as well as sponsoring their own sports teams. In the summer of 1950, the Hudson Scott sports team travelled to London to take part alongside twenty-one others in the annual Metal Box national sports day.

But with the cost of living and unemployment going in the wrong direction, and with the social housing waiting list also on the increase, there was little feelgood factor permeating the country.

Things came to a head with the 'Cost of Living' General Election of 1950. An incredible 83.9 per cent of people eligible to vote did so in February 1950; such was the interest in national politics and the desire to drive change and improvement. (To put this into context, the turn out figures in the three elections since the turn of the twenty first century has just scraped over the 60 per cent mark.)

It wasn't just the domestic political landscape that had changed since the war either. Much to Churchill's horror following his General Election defeat in 1945, the British Empire started to deconstruct in favour of a more politically correct Commonwealth. To promote and develop the concept of equals rather than colonial minions, bi-annual meetings of Commonwealth premiers took place in London.

One of the outcomes of these early conferences was Australia's launching of an immigration programme aimed at increasing the population of the country, improving the skills amongst the workforce, and expanding the economy. And if it offered an interesting alternative to tens of thousands of displaced, downtrodden Europeans in the process, then all the better. By the end of 1950 it was reported that 124,000 job vacancies existed down under. (It would be the start of the mass migration that continued over the following two decades.)

At the election, Clemente Atlee was returned again but with a much reduced majority. The generation who had experienced terrible deprivation and loss, and who had learned to despise waste – whether that consisted of food, money or time – decided to give Labour another chance. But Atlee knew the clock continued to tick.

The only other thing that provided the post-war (predominantly male) generation with a little escapism from such an austere existence was football. If golf, tennis and rugby were elitist, then football was the working man's game and firms recognised this – they all had their own football teams (and cricket teams in the summer). A thriving amateur league also took place every Thursday afternoon, which was half-day closing in the city. And when the young men of the city weren't actually *playing* football, they were watching it.

One schoolboy who was a keen fan was Gerald Irwin who, through his father's connections, landed a plumb job:

> My dad was friendly with someone in the Carlisle United Shareholders' Association and he got me a job selling programmes. It was great as I got to see games every week, the first team one week, the reserves the next. I sold programmes until I went into the army in 1951.

Even as a young lad, Gerald also remembers some of the more entrepreneurial policies adopted by the Association:

> I was never quite sure how it worked. I have a feeling the money [from the programmes] went to the Shareholders' Association and not to the club. All the programmes were numbered and they used to have a competition where they awarded a prize for the 'winning' programme. The story goes that the way they chose it was to pick one of the programmes that hadn't been sold! I don't know if that is true but certainly I didn't know of anyone who won the prize.

By the half-way point of the twentieth century, Carlisle United had been in existence for forty-six years. The club moved from its humble homes at Milhome Bank and then at Devonshire Park, to the slightly less humble ground at Brunton Park in 1909. League status was achieved for the club in 1928.

With flat caps, collar and ties, and dark overcoats being the order of the day, thousands would trudge down Warwick Road to watch the Blues play.

Strong evidence to suggest football was the main post-war leisure activity comes when the average gates are considered. Before the war gates at Brunton Park hovered between five and six thousand. In the first season following, the average gate was over ten thousand and never dropped below five figures until season 1952–53.

Claude Daley was never a big football fan; instead he enjoyed his horse racing, working as a bookies' clerk in his spare time for local bookmakers, Willie Little and 'Soss' Norman. Claude's son Paul however *was* a fan, and was going to Brunton Park even at that early age, with his friends, brothers Gerald and Gordon Reardon. Among Paul's earliest recollections was him attending the club's first big post-war game against Leeds United in the FA Cup. Leeds were a good Second Division team who boasted among their number a promising young Welsh player called John Charles. The Yorkshire club ran out 5–2 winners in the game but Carlisle had the financial consolation of enjoying their biggest ever gate – almost 23,000.

One fan who typified the commitment to the local team was George Baxter. George was a charge-hand at 14MU, who served in the war as an aerial gunner in the RAF, and who participated in 28 bombing raids over Germany.

George followed the blues home and away from childhood. He recalled one bizarre trip to Rotherham immediately after the war:

> I went down in a cattle truck, standing all the way from ten o'clock at night till six the next morning with three sheep and a cow. At the match I had to stand alone because I still smelled of the animals!

The then player manager Ivor Broadis spotted the regular hitch-hiking fan and made him a semi-official club mascot. City-wide recognition soon followed and George ended up travelling with the team to away games.

For decades following, his party-piece would be to run on to the field with his stuffed fox – Olga – before home games; his distinctive staccato run earning him the affectionate nickname of 'Twinkletoes' or 'Twinks' for short.

To summarise then, our parents and grandparents led an extremely austere existence! But something was about to happen that would give them all a distraction that would fire their imagination and give them a few weeks' escape from rationing, politics and hard work.

Little did they know that Carlisle United were about to be drawn against Arsenal (the biggest football club in Europe) in the FA Cup (the oldest cup competition in the world). Moreover, United's charismatic young manager succeeded in having everyone believe that we were going to beat them!

THIS IS YOUR MANAGER SPEAKING

When they close the book on football managers and enter into the great debate about who was the best, the man who built Liverpool into the club that is known globally today will undoubtedly be in the top four or five.

But before most people at Anfield had even heard of Bill Shankly – the manager – the Scot was embarking on his first managerial position at Brunton Park, Carlisle. Thus Shankly's unique place in Carlisle United's history was assured, as for the second time in his professional career, the Cumbrian club became his starting point south of the border – first as a player in 1932, then as a manager in March 1949.

William Shankly was born on 2 September 1913, in the mining village of Glenbuck, Ayrshire; the second youngest (and youngest boy) of John and Barbara Shankly's ten children (five boys and five girls). For such a small village, Glenbuck was known for its conveyor belt of young footballers, produced mainly by its junior team, the Glenbuck Cherrypickers. Over fifty young Glenbuck players played senior football throughout the British Isles and North America – they included seven who were capped for Scotland.

As far as the Shankly household was concerned, the boys inherited their footballing skills from their maternal side – their mother being a member of the celebrated Blyth family. Two of Barbara's brothers played professionally. Bob for Glasgow Rangers, Middlesbrough, Preston and Dundee before ending as player/manager at Portsmouth. Her other brother, William, meanwhile, also played for Preston and Portsmouth before becoming director and then chairman at none other than Carlisle United.

With such a pedigree, it is not surprising that all five Shankly brothers were destined to become professional footballers. 'Little Willie,' as he was known to his family, initially started down the mines upon leaving school but when the mines closed, he became redundant.

His eldest brother Alec had played with Ayr United and Clyde; next eldest Jimmy was the first Shankly to sign for Carlisle United; he moved on to Sheffield United and Southend before moving back north, first to Barrow and then back to Brunton Park to end his career.

John Shankly played for Portsmouth, Luton, Halifax, Coventry and Alloa; while Bob spent seventeen years with Falkirk.

At 16, Bill was too young to sign for the Cherrypickers, but not so young as to sign for the nearby Cronberry Juniors. Ever the experimenter and innovator, among Shankly's armoury at that young age was the virtually unseen skill of the long throw-in. (*He would practice by throwing balls over houses in the village!*)

It was when he was with Cronberry that local scout Peter Carruthers spotted him playing. Carruthers had contacts with most Scottish and northern English clubs and knew what each of them were looking for. He recommended the right-half to the young man's uncle Bill Blyth and Carlisle. As a result, Shankly was invited to follow in his brother Jimmy's footsteps for trials at Brunton Park in August 1932. He later recalled his first impressions:

> I came to Carlisle United as a boy 32 years ago and at that time it was a hencoop, a glorified hencoop. The stand and terraces and everything about the ground were in a terrible condition, except for the pitch, and that was always a good one.

His first game was on a hot Saturday afternoon and Carlisle trainer Tom Curry had to play alongside the young right-half because of a lack of personnel. The game was against Middlesbrough reserves, who proceeded to take the makeshift Carlisle side apart. A dejected Shankly and his teammates trudged off the field at the end having been hammered 6-0. But

Curry had taken to the youngster immediately – he liked what he saw close up and had no hesitation in recommending his services to manager Billy Hampson.

Tom Curry became an early influence on Shankly, building confidence (*yes, even Bill Shankly needed confidence-building at times*) and developing the skills that quickly propelled him to the brink of the first team. (Tom developed a reputation for nurturing young talent and was picked up by Matt Busby to help develop his 'Busby Babes'. Tragically, Curry died in the Munich air disaster of 1958.)

Shankly started the season in the reserves, who played in the North Eastern League against top quality non-League sides, as well as the reserve teams from the three North East giants. He made his first team debut on the final day of 1932 in a 2–2 draw against Rochdale.

By the end of the 1932–33 season, he had won his first medal in professional football when the reserves beat Newcastle United reserves 1–0 in the final of the North Eastern League Cup (it was a prize Shankly treasured throughout his life). He had also established himself as a first team regular and a fans' favourite, with his never-say-die attitude on the field. Unknown to him at the time, he had come to the attention of Preston North End who offered Carlisle £500 for the Scot's services before the season was even over. With Carlisle about to embark on their annual close-season clear out, and with £500 being £500, they felt it was an opportunity too good to pass up for a young lad who had only played half a season.

Initially enthused by the thought of moving to a top club with eyes on the First Division and on cup success, when it came to negotiating the transfer, Shankly actually turned Preston down (something that became a bit of a trait). He was becoming a big fish in the Carlisle pond, whereas he was an unknown quantity at Preston, where he would undoubtedly spend most of his time in the reserves. But after persuasion from his brother Alec, Shankly had a change of heart and decided to move to Deepdale after all.

In later life he recalled how fortunate he was to be in such a profession. And despite his initial reservations about the move to Preston, he spoke of his obvious ambition and how a move to a bigger club was inevitable:

At the end of the season I was paid £4 10s a week, which was good, because the top rate in English football then was £8. I was much better off than the coalminer for doing something in the fresh air that I would have done for nothing. But Carlisle was only a stepping stone. I knew I was going further than that.

The Carlisle fans were in uproar when the news broke about the transfer.

History repeated itself as far as Shankly's Preston career began; as with his time at Brunton Park a year earlier, he played his first game in the reserves in August 1933 but he found himself in the first team before the year was out.

The youngster quickly formed a great partnership with former England International Bob Kelly and established himself as one of the most exciting young talents in the country. Notwithstanding pre-war communication limitations, news of his progress travelled fast round the football community and before the season was out, Portsmouth and Arsenal both made enquiries about Preston's new right-half. Arsenal were the First Division Champions (more of that later) but their overtures were rebuffed by the club who saw their young star as an asset, as they sought promotion to the top flight.

That promotion was duly secured during Shankly's first full season in the first team (1933–34) but with his friend and partner Kelly now on the wrong side of forty, it was suggested *he* take his career in a different direction and he duly took up the role of player/manager of…*Carlisle United!*

Following Kelly's departure, and with some new signings to enhance the Lilywhites' squad, the Lancashire club set about establishing themselves with a series of strong campaigns in both cup and league:

1934–35 – 10th in the league; quarter finals of the FA Cup
1935–36 – 7th in the league; fourth round of the FA Cup
1936–37 –14th in the league; FA Cup runners-up

The following season was even more successful when Preston came within a game of achieving the League and Cup double: it was (*who else?*) Arsenal who beat them at Deepdale to clinch another League title on the final day of the season, but Shankly and his colleagues recovered quickly to bounce back from the previous year's disappointment against Sunderland to beat Huddersfield Town at Wembley and win the FA Cup for the first time in since 1889 (when the club completed the League and Cup double.)

With his Preston teammates after winning the Cup in 1948

Proud Scottish International

It was the pinnacle of Shankly's playing career and was matched the same month when he returned to Wembley to win his first international cap against the *auld enemy*.

With Shankly now in the prime of his career, war broke out and the Football League and Football Association concluded that the League programme should be cancelled and players' contracts should be suspended. Seven mini leagues were formed and cup competitions were organised with teams from within fifty miles of one another.

In 1940 Shankly joined the RAF and was initially posted to Warrington, from where he continued his Preston career. He therefore took part in North End's successful 1940–41 season that saw them win the North Regional League title.

Not only that, the Deepdale club made it to Wembley to play in the Football League Cup Final – a replacement for the FA Cup which saw regional finalists play off. Their opponents in the 'Cup Final'? Yes, you've guessed it, Arsenal. Playing with Shankly in the Preston team by now was the man who would become the greatest Lilywhite of them all – Tom Finney.

Shankly playing for Preston against Arsenal in the Football League Cup Final in 1941

The Wembley final took place in front of 60,000 and finished 1–1. The replay at Ewood Park saw the Lancastrians (*containing eight Scots!*) run out 2–1 winners.

As players were being called up, they were being stationed all over the country (and obviously sent overseas in some cases). This resulted in organised football becoming increasingly disorganised as players regularly 'guested' for other teams.

Some of these player/team combinations make for fascinating musings for the football historian: Blackpool greats Matthews and Mortenson playing for Arsenal; Stan Cullis and Frank Swift playing for Liverpool; Charlie Buchan and Matt Busby playing for Chelsea.

The war also accelerated the careers of future greats who would become synonymous with the club they debuted for – like Finney at Preston, Jackie Milburn at Newcastle and Nat Lofthouse at Bolton.

And then there were incongruous pairings where lower league teams couldn't believe their good fortune: Joe Mercer playing for Reading; Tommy Lawton and Andy Beattie for Aldershot; Leslie Compton for Chester to name but a few.

By 1942 Deepdale had been commandeered for military purposes and Shankly's various postings around the country saw him guest for Bolton, Cardiff, Liverpool, Luton, Norwich and…*Arsenal*. It was becoming uncanny the number of times the paths of the Scottish right-half and the London giants were crossing. Shankly couldn't fail to be impressed by the country's top club:

> Arsenal were the kings of the 1930s of course. They had everything: the marble halls of Highbury, and aluminium massage baths for the players. Arsenal thought big.

But this latest liaison was to end in acrimony and leave Shankly with a bitter feeling towards the Gunners.

He had played a major part in Arsenal winning the Football League Southern Championship and reaching the 1943 League Cup Southern

Final that was to be played at Wembley. Prior to the final however, Arsenal recalled most of their excellent 'pre-war' regulars from around the country and dropped their 'guest' players – Shankly among them.

Arsenal hammered Charlton 7–1 in the Final – Shankly never forgave them.

When the war ended normal service was resumed as far as far as the league and cup competitions were concerned. Stadia were packed for the start of the 1946–47 season, as demobilised fans attempted to escape the horrors of the war years and return to normality.

For many of the demobilised players it was a different story. Many were among the tens of thousands who had paid the ultimate price, while many others had seen what should have been the peaks of their careers snatched away from them during the conflict.

Bill Shankly himself was perhaps a classic example: he was now in his mid-thirties with a wife, a child and a dodgy knee. The reception he received from the Preston hierarchy was cool; Shankly would need all of his tenacity and unswerving self-belief to prove them wrong.

He soldiered on for another couple of seasons before being told at the start of the 1948–49 that the club were looking to youth for the future and his first-team services were no longer required.

Instead, he was offered the job of coaching the reserve and youth team players at the club; he reluctantly accepted the role and took a correspondence course in physiotherapy as well as gaining a coaching certificate with the FA. Over the following months, he made representation to the club that he should receive a retirement benefit after his sixteen-year service and 300-plus games. The toing-and-froing between the two parties rumbled on into early 1949 before the directors – knowing that other clubs were interested in taking him in a player-manager role – made a final offer of a testimonial on the condition that he stay at Deepdale in the reserve coach/physio role for three years. Shankly was furious.

Eighty miles north of Deepdale, and sixteen years after the Scot had left the club, Carlisle United was still a tiny spec on the horizon of English football. Its only notable claim to fame came through its recent player/manager.

During the war, top amateur player Ivor Broadis had guested for Tottenham Hotspur, having played a few games for Manchester United prior to war breaking out.

Still in the service at the end of the war, Broadis lined up for Spurs against Wolves as competitive football resumed in August 1946. Within a few of weeks of the new season however, Broadis was posted to Crosby-on-Eden just outside Carlisle, and his dream of starting his professional career at White Hart Lane was over.

When the Brunton Park club found out that there was such a talent on their doorstep, they made the unprecedented move of offering the 23-year-old the position of player/manager. As the offer coincided with Broadis being demobbed, and impressed by the enthusiasm of directors John Miller and John Corrieri, Ivor decided to take the job.

By season 1948–49 Broadis, the player, was being recognised as a hot property; this coupled with Ivor's frustration at the Board's lack of ambition led to him 'transferring himself' to Sunderland for £18,000 in January 1949. Ivor is always keen to clarify the move today:

> The inference is that I could do a better deal for myself, 'selling myself' (the player), by 'myself' (the manager). The truth is that I did no more than any player of that era was allowed to do, which was simply that I decided which club I wanted to join (there were several in for me). The secretary and the board handled the fee and the financial discussion with the interested clubs.

The club advertised for a replacement and received forty applicants – among them was their former player, Bill Shankly. There then followed a rather odd few weeks before the appointment was made.

The Carlisle board didn't make life particularly easy for themselves by quickly whittling the applicants down to just two – Shankly and Bobby Gurney, the former Sunderland centre-forward and [then] current manager of Hordon Colliery Welfare.

Interviews took place in early February 1949, and the directors made their provisional offer known to both applicants, but an appointment was deferred, as the two were asked to return to their clubs and confirm the ability to gain release from their respective contracts. They agreed to meet again two weeks later.

The position was made known to the local press and it was stated that – rather bizarrely – should the chosen candidate not accept the position, it did not automatically follow that the other would be appointed. Instead, another shortlist may be drawn up, that would include the name of the other candidate!

This is exactly what happened.

Shortly before the second meeting, Shankly informed the club that he could not agree to the terms offered and he therefore wished no longer to be considered. The befuddled directors met as scheduled and after much huffing and puffing, activated the clause outlined in their previous statement and declared no suitable candidate. Instead they announced their intention to draw up an amended shortlist that *would* include the name of Bobby Gurney. (*You couldn't make it up, could you?*)

Of course, when Carlisle approached other clubs – all now moving into the key last third of the season – they were given short shrift. Moreover, did they honestly think that the applicants they had discarded were now going to re-apply?

By the middle of March, the board were in an impossible position – effectively no one wanted the job. They decided to meet on Tuesday 22 March 1949 to discuss a way forward and whether it was appropriate to offer the position to Gurney (not that anyone was sure if he would even want it now).

At five o'clock, barely two hours before the meeting convened, Bill Shankly called the club and asked the board of directors if they would consider him for the position after all. Five weeks after their interviews therefore, it was a decision between hiring Shankly or Gurney.

You would have thought the directors would have been relieved to receive Shankly's call wouldn't you? Apparently not – when a vote was taken, the decision who to appoint was split.

Cue, more harrumphing.

Finally, a second vote was taken and Bill Shankly was the unanimous choice. The following day, club secretary Bill Clark telephoned Shankly to offer him the position. Much to everyone's relief – shortly before the team were due to kick-off against Hull City that night – he accepted. A full seven weeks after Ivor Broadis transferred to Sunderland, Carlisle had a new manager.

The appointment appears to have been universally popular. It's a truism in football that you can never con the fans, and both the supporters of Preston and Carlisle wished their former playing hero well, while his contemporaries in the game recognised the talent he would bring in his new role.

The only party not to support the move appeared to be the Preston board who withdrew their offer of a benefit match. This left Shankly – a man of high principles – bitter, as he later wrote in his autobiography:

> I felt the people who were running Preston at the time had cheated me out of my benefit match and that was the biggest let down of my life in football. It didn't need that to happen like that. If I promise you something, you'll get it.

Shankly travelled to watch his new charges play their next game against Barrow on the Saturday following, and then took charge for the final eight games of the season and won the Cumberland Cup to boot.

Upon his arrival back at the club that he left fifteen years earlier, he discovered that little had changed by way of facilities and infrastructure. He and his wife Ness moved into a club house on Tullie Street, just a few hundred yards from Brunton Park. This close proximity meant he was never away; he set about re-painting and repairing the sad ground.

His natural enthusiasm and 'can do' attitude was infectious and the fans responded accordingly. These were the days of 'community' and with little other leisure activity available the local football club became the focal point for many. Nowhere more so than a remote outpost like Carlisle, and by involving spectators in their club and inviting the press to regular briefings,

Shankly was already becoming the Pied Piper figure the football world would recognise in later years. He reflected on his return to Carlisle in his autobiography at the end of his career:

> I had the knowledge. I had been with people who knew how to train teams and I had my own conception of human beings and psychology. I took all the training and played in the practice matches, did the scouting, cleaned the boots, brushed out the bloody dressing room, everything. I even burned all the training kit. It was an absolute disgrace, it was stinking, so I got a big furnace and burned the lot. The players got everything new and what we couldn't get, we ordered.

By the time of Shankly's first full season in charge (1949–50) crowds in excess of fifteen thousand were flocking to Brunton Park, sensing that the club were on the brink of something big with this charismatic manager at the helm. (The crowds were larger than those enjoyed by the club in the First Division in the mid-1970s). Gates of six and seven thousand were commonplace for reserve team matches.

Shankly, in turn, responded by taking over the tannoy twenty minutes before kick-off: "This is your manager speaking…" he would announce, before going on to explain his team selection, his thoughts on the most recent performance, and his expectations this afternoon. Conscious of the community spirit that existed at clubs like Carlisle, he would round off his pre-game rallying cry with:

> The boys are going to give their best – I'll make sure of that. There are one or two local lads in the team, so make sure you cheer them on.

(Paddy Waters was a team mate of Shankly's at Preston, and someone who would follow him to Brunton Park during the 1950–51 season. He knew Shankly from old and said he always used to end his speech with "And may the best team win!" and then under his breath mutter, "*as long as it's us!*")

Once back in the dressing room, the psychology would continue with his players, stressing that the opposition:

> …have had to travel hundreds of miles to get to Fortress Brunton – they'll be exhausted. They won't have experienced supporters like ours, who are the best I've ever seen.

He brought new ideas to training – endurance road-running was replaced by stamina-building exercise, and running up and down terraces was replaced by ball-work. He negotiated with the board and part-time players' employers to allow the local lads to participate in sessions with their full-time colleagues. (This had been a constant frustration for Shankly's predecessor, Ivor Broadis, who had to endure his part-time players training in mid-week in pitch darkness.) Such commitment was reciprocated by his players. Paddy Waters later summed up the atmosphere around the club:

> There was a great team spirit at Carlisle and always a competition to keep your place. Shankly has always had a good reserve team wherever he's been and it makes for a very determined side. It was just the same at Carlisle in the early fifties. The place was really buzzing while Shanks was in charge.

Although then playing for Sunderland, Ivor Broadis still lived in Carlisle having married a local girl. He continued to train with Carlisle United before travelling east each week to play for the Wearsiders. He gives a fascinating insight to Shankly's mind-set:

> Shankly's philosophy was 'You must come off the training pitch knackered. If you put enough in, you will get enough out' He would ask what I was doing in the afternoon and invite me to come down to play one-on-one in the car park with two chimney pots. You had

to knock the chimney pots over to score. I soon learned that if you didn't let him win we'd be there till midnight!

The two were good friends but Shankly wanted no one to be in any doubt who was boss. Despite Ivor performing excellently for Sunderland and getting close to the England team, he was torn off a strip by Shankly one morning when he arrived late for training, "What do you think you're doing? Who do you think you are?" But his admiration for Broadis was obvious when he later described him as, "…one of the strongest and most dangerous inside-forwards that ever played."

Shankly's regard for the game was absolute. Paddy Waters's wife Doreen remembers her [then] future husband recalling his first few months in Carlisle:

> Paddy and Alex McCue used to lodge with Winnie Howard on Warwick Road when they first came. There was a lady staying there who was very sedate and – referring to Shankly – she used to say, 'if that man is coming here to talk about football again, tell me and I'll go up to my room!' Shankly just talked about football all the time. He thought everyone should talk about football. But there was a great atmosphere when Shankly was here. There was a great camaraderie among the players. He was just like the players. He wasn't aloof and that's why I think the players had so much respect for him.

One of the most remarkable stories about Shankly came just after the Arsenal tie in January 1951. His success at the tiny club had caught the attention of none other than First Division Liverpool, who had themselves suffered a cup upset at the hands of Norwich City on the same day. With their manager George Kay having resigned due to ill-health, the Anfield club approached Shankly and asked if he would like to be interviewed for the position.

The Liverpool board clearly had not done their homework on the Scot – they suggested at the interview that they would scrutinize the manager's team selection and reserved the right to alter it if they saw fit. Shankly asked, "If I don't pick the team, what am I manager of?" Upon hearing a few days later that the post had been offered to Don Welsh, Brighton and Hove Albion's manager, Shankly's barbed comment was, "He got the job because he is in the masons."

(Liverpool never did find the right formula and were relegated to the Second Division in 1954. They came looking for Shankly again in 1959 when he was manager of Huddersfield Town. The rest, as they say…)

THE BOYS IN BLUE

As Paddy Waters suggested, Shankly's mantra was to build up a good team spirit amongst his players, whilst at the same time developing a squad made up of tried and trusted veterans alongside emerging youngsters, which would generate competition for places in the process. When he arrived at Carlisle he set about assessing the squad he had inherited and making the right additions with the £18,000 windfall the club had received from Sunderland for his predecessor Ivor Broadis.

By the turn of the year during the 1950–51 season, Shankly had built a good squad, good enough to rival anything in the two divisions that made up the third tier of the Football League. Most of Shankly's twenty-plus players had featured in the first team but by the time of the third round of the FA Cup, injuries had taken their toll and the manager was almost down to the bare bones, in terms of numbers.

It is often assumed by the casual United historian that the eleven players who played in the Arsenal tie (the same eleven played in both games) were Shankly's first choice eleven; they have gone down in Carlisle United folklore, with many supporters who have studied the history of the club, naming them off the top of their heads, pub-quiz style. But what is not widely known is that the two games in question are the *only* time the eleven ever played together.

It would probably be unfair to label the team a hotchpotch outfit but they *were* a mixture of regulars, squad players, new signings and part-timers.

In the 'regular' category comes goalkeeper Jim MacLaren who joined on a free transfer in late 1948, after his friend and former teammate Phil Turner recommended him to the [then] manager Ivor Broadis. MacLaren made his debut on New Year's Day 1949 against Southport. From March 1950 the keeper started a run of 200-plus successive games over the following four years (still a club record for consecutive appearances).

Jim was born in Crieff, Perthshire in 1921. Like many of his generation he was a good all-round sportsman as a boy and excelled at both football and golf (he later told his daughter that he should have taken up golf instead, as golfers had a longer career!). But like *all* of his generation, his ambitions were halted by the war and MacLaren served in the Scots Guards, seeing action as a tank driver in Central Europe.

Towards the end of the war he was stationed near Chester and when the conflict finally ended, he jumped at the chance of a trial with the Seals. He impressed manager Frank Brown enough to be offered a professional contract and he played thirty times for the Sealand Road club before receiving the call from the Cumbrians.

To say that goalkeeping was in his blood is an understatement – he was one of four brothers who kept goal professionally.

One of MacLaren's best friends in the team was right-back Alex McIntosh (or McTosh as the players called him). Born in Inverurie in 1923, he first played for Dundee before moving south of the border to join Barrow after the war. He was considered by many to be one of the best full-backs in the division and had come to the attention of Shankly towards the end of the 1948–49 season. The Carlisle manager made his move in September 1949 and convinced McIntosh to move back nearer to the border with the promise of a push for promotion to the higher leagues.

He proved to be an unassuming player, coasting through games with his astute positional play and crisp tackling. The home crowd would grow to appreciate McIntosh's steadying influence over the following five seasons.

McIntosh's full-back partner for the big game was popular local lad Norman Coupe. Norman was born in the small village of Cumwhinton, near Carlisle in 1922.

Serving in the Royal Marines during the war, he was one of the part time players at the club, splitting his time between football and panel beating at the County Garage. Coupe was a good example of a local part-timer who was happy with his lot. Financially, it worked out well for his like: a time-served tradesman could earn in excess of £5 per week; as a semi-professional with the club, he would earn another £8 a week, training Tuesdays and Thursdays, and playing on a Saturday. With a £1 bonus for a draw and £2 for a win many local lads had no desire to go full time because it simply didn't pay.

Coupe was never a regular in the team but he had enjoyed a run in the side prior to the third-round FA Cup tie. The man he kept out of the side enjoyed a far more illustrious career, but many modern-day supporters have never heard of him!

Alec Scott actually played in the FA Cup Final eighteen months earlier for Leicester City against Wolves. He switched foxes and joined Carlisle in the close season following his Wembley appearance and ended up playing 200 games for the Cumbrians during a seven-year career. Alas he was destined to be outdone in the history books by Norman Coupe's modest 31 appearances, due to the fact that Norman played in *the* game.

The defensive unit was marshalled by the young centre-half Geoff Twentyman. Like Coupe, 'Twent' was a local lad and like Coupe, he spent his amateur career with Swifts Rovers. How he came to be involved in football in the first place however is perhaps the most interesting story of all.

Twentyman was the son of a farmer from Brampton and was a strapping lad from childhood. He became Cumberland wrestling champion in successive years at the age of 14 and 15. By this time however he was also a keen soccer player, having stumbled into the football world on New Year's Day 1937, aged seven.

He was helping his dad transport some sheep through Carlisle when they were making their way home past Brunton Park. Unknown to the lad, Carlisle United were playing York City and the roar from the crowd as the teams took to the pitch ahead of the match, excited the youngster so much he asked his father if they could go and see what was going on.

What *was* going on would have a lasting effect on the young boy and would shape the rest of his life and career. Once inside the father and son encountered complete silence: the crowd of were observing a minute's silence out of respect for United's popular centre-half Jack Round who had died days earlier after having suffered a burst appendix following a cup tie against Stockport County in late November. Following the period of silence the crowd and players spontaneously broke into singing *Abide with Me*. The moving experience struck a chord with young Geoff whose own brother died in a shooting accident a few years earlier.

From then on he was obsessed with football and developed his skills by challenging anyone who would take part in a farmyard kick-around.

By the time he was 16, he was starting to attract the attention of local scouts, one of whom told the [then] United manager Ivor Broadis about the young lad. Ivor recalls his first impressions:

> I first saw Geoff playing in the Carlisle and District League for Swifts at the age of 16. I'd heard he was a champion wrestler but I was surprised to see he had a natural ability with both feet. I know he was very proud of that because there were few players had such ability back then. The only thing Geoff didn't have to his game in those early days was acceleration over the first 15 yards, but we managed to improve his speed in time.

Broadis arranged with the chairman – who happened to be the boss of the local Ford dealers – to give young Twentyman an apprenticeship as a panel beater (again, like Norman Coupe). This placated the lad's parents who were concerned about his future should he not make the grade; Broadis then set about shaping the rough diamond. Twentyman made his Carlisle debut in the final game of the 1946–47 season at Chester City where they lost heavily 4–0; the one plus point was the performance of the 17-year-old debutant who promised much for the future.

By the time of Shankly's arrival, Twentyman was a regular and the Scot saw the young man as an integral part of his plans. He switched him from wing-half to centre-half and made him captain of the team (although McIntosh assumed the latter role by the time of the Arsenal tie).

His career threatened to stall however when he was called up for national service shortly after the Arsenal tie. Stationed at Oswestry, Twentyman had only been there a matter of days when he was summoned to his Camp Adjutant's office to be asked: "Gunner Twentyman does the name Shankly mean anything to you?"

In a stroke of breathtaking effrontery, Shankly had contacted the War Office and told them that Carlisle United could win the Third Division North providing the army could release Twentyman on a regular basis.

"We've decided to let you go," continued Twentyman's superior, "but once you're out of the running, it will stop!"

Twentyman was viewed by many who saw him play as a big strong man, but he was the first to point out that he wasn't the strongest in the squad – that accolade went to half-back Paddy Waters.

By the time of the Arsenal tie, Paddy had only been with the club a month, having signed from Preston in late November 1950.

Waters was born in Dublin in January 1922. His early career was spent in his homeland and culminated in his winning the Inter City Cup with Bohemians in 1945. He won international honours in a 1–0 victory over Wales the following year. In 1947 he moved to the mainland and joined Preston North End, where he played alongside Bill Shankly. Shankly once said of Waters, "He could run like a hare, and tackle like a bear, he was as good a defender as there was."

The first Carlisle manager to look at Waters with view to his signature was Ivor Broadis two years before he actually signed. With Shankly in the manager's seat in 1950, he went back to Preston to convince the brave halfback to follow him north; his next task was to persuade him to stay – Waters later described his first impressions of Brunton Park:

> It was just like a big wooden rabbit hutch. The facilities were shocking, especially for someone like me who'd been used to Preston's ground. I was all ready to pack my bags and get the first train back to Lancashire but Bill persuaded me to stay. What I would say mind you is that although the club were struggling financially, the support

was amazing. We were in the Third Division North and pulling in an average home gate of 16,000. My first home match was against Southport in front of 17,000 people when we won 2–0.

Brunton Park in 1950

Like Shankly, Paddy was a non-drinker but there was an exception to this rule in the form of his pre-game ritual. Before every match he would break a raw egg into a glass and top it up with sherry. Neither shaken, nor stirred, he would just neck the concoction in one gulp. His wife used to say he was breaking his pledge but Paddy would reply, "No that's different – it's medicinal!" (*No wonder he could run like a hare and tackle like a bear!*)

Waters made his United debut along with (and alongside) Tommy Kinloch. Kinloch was a squad player who was brought in during the close season; Shankly travelled north to Falkirk to persuade his brother Bob – who was managing the Brookville Road club at the time – to part with the right-half.

Shankly had been struggling with the half-back positions for most of the season and Kinloch and Waters promised much as United ran out 2–1 winners against a strong Stockport County side on 2 December 1950.

The gap at inside-forward left by Ivor Broadis (the player) was enormous and throughout his tenure, Shankly tried different players in the positions. The one player who was a regular in the role was someone who was signed by Broadis and who played alongside him before he left.

Phil Turner was born in Frodsham, Cheshire in 1927 and was signed from Chester City as a 20-year-old for £625. (It was Turner who recommended his old team mate Jim MacLaren to Broadis when the Carlisle manager was looking for a new goalkeeper.)

Turner came with a reputation for possessing an electrifying pace: 'Carlisle's Jessie Owens!' he was dubbed by one local journalist. But an even greater attribute was his ability to run on to the ball at his speed and assume instant control, which usually resulted in panic in the opposing box.

Turner was a prolific scorer for Carlisle in his own right (averaging a goal every three games), but another key feature of play was his capacity to link up with the several other Blues he played alongside in the United forward line during his three years at the club. His goal-assists and overall contribution therefore throughout his time at Brunton Park cannot be overstated.

One of the many forwards Turner played alongside was yet another sporting serviceman – Bill Caton.

Today, one of the great catchphrases of officialdom is that 'we are all in this together.' Whatever the validity of such modern-day claims, there is no doubt that the phrase applied to everyone living in the '40s and '50s. It didn't matter what someone's background was, or what their occupation was, men of a certain age invariably ended up in the forces. Bill Caton ended up in the Royal Artillery.

Like Carlisle fruit merchant and fan Sapper Claude Daley, and Carr's Biscuits' magnate Captain Richard Carr (and Steve McQueen for that matter), Gunner Bill Caton was captured by the Germans and became a Prisoner Of War. And like Claude Daley (but unlike Richard Carr and Steve McQueen), this particular hero, managed to escape his captors and return home.

He left the army in 1947 and joined his local club Stoke City. Two years later he became part of the Shankly revolution at Brunton Park.

Caton distinguished himself on the field by becoming one of the early exponents of the long throw – something Shankly himself had perfected in his playing days, and something the manager encouraged the inside-forward to utilise at every opportunity. Caton however, was destined to miss the Arsenal tie through injury, and would find it hard to wrestle his place back from the man who took it – Jimmy Jackson.

Jackson was a Glaswegian, born on New Year's Day in 1921 and following the war, started his professional career south of the border with Bolton Wanderers in 1947. He played a mere eleven games for the Trotters before Shankly signed him for the Cumbrians in the close season of 1950. Jackson went on to play in a hundred games across five seasons at Carlisle and – with his speed and clever link-up play – became another player to be highly thought of by the fans.

Someone who played half that number, and yet probably earned even greater affection from the home fans, was another one of their own – Eric 'Spud' Hayton who started his playing career with the club during the war when he worked on the railway. Signing semi-professional forms in 1946, Spud went on to play a modest forty-nine games over the next six years.

He started his early career as a winger but developed into a bit of a utility player: outside or inside-forward, left-half, or anywhere else he was needed. When Geoff Twentyman and later Paddy Waters were both available, Spud would revert to the role of travelling reserve. Spud was renowned for his bite in the tackle, his honesty and loyalty to his team and the game, all qualities that Shankly demanded and as such – despite his utility role – was greatly admired by the boss.

Another player with the same ethos, which in turn resulted in the same level of admiration from his manager, was centre-forward Jackie Lindsay.

Like Shankly, Jackie was a Scot and the two had such a close relationship, the player got away with calling his manager 'Hector' (Shankly also called Lindsay 'Hector'. *No one, including Jackie's son John, knows why!*)

Lindsay was actually signed by Shankly's predecessor Ivor Broadis. Ivor describes him as "the biggest bargain ever," following his £300 capture from Bury in August 1947. He had arrived at Bury from Sheffield Wednesday for whom he played in the top flight.

Lindsay was older than his new manager (Broadis) but the two were destined to strike up an effective partnership for Carlisle before the player-manager moved to Sunderland.

The lean, strong front man made an immediate impact scoring twice on his league debut in a 4–2 win over Darlington. He then endeared himself further to the home crowd by scoring fourteen goals in nine games, including four in one game against Crewe.

Lindsay – with his tenacious running – went on to prove the perfect foil for the elegant Broadis and between them they wracked up 46 leagues goals between them in their short time together.

If Lindsay was a Broadis signing, another Shankly capture was that of George Dick, brought in to compete with the other front-men in 1948. Like Jim MacLaren, George Dick was a proud member of the Scots Guards and the British Army Of the Rhine during the war. Like many other of his contemporaries, he was also a good all-round sportsman, excelling in boxing before securing a trial with Blackpool in August 1946.

Their manager Joe Smith signed the forward immediately and he made a scoring debut that season against Arsenal (*who else?*). He was with the Seasiders for two years and his spell there culminated in him playing the FA Cup Final against Manchester United in 1948, alongside Mortenson and Matthews.

(Carlisle therefore had two players in the 1950–51 squad who had played in an FA Cup Final – George Dick and Alec Scott. *Neither of them was destined to play in the Arsenal tie however!*)

Blackpool sold George to West Ham in 1948 and he became one of Shankly's first big signings during the close-season a year later. For his first full season, Shankly installed him as club captain.

(Dick was followed a few weeks later from Blackpool by yet another Scot, half-back Tommy Buchan, who would only be at the club for a season playing thirty games before moving on.)

The supply to the front-men was provided by probably the best player in the squad.

In 1982, the local newspaper had a poll to decide the club's greatest ever player. The man who won it was Billy Hogan.

Billy was a Salford lad, born in January 1924. Playing his early amateur football in the Lancashire leagues, he fought in Italy during the war before returning home to Manchester.

The only thing missing from the wide-man's armoury was the ability to head the ball. There remains today some confusion as to why this is. The suggestion amongst many fans is that Hogan had a metal plate fitted in his head following a war injury, which prevented him from heading the heavy, leather ball. This however, was denied by the man himself when he spoke to United historian David Steele some years later; he simply commented that heading the ball gave him terrible headaches and therefore he ducked out of the aerial game for his own comfort.

No doubt, there are some younger fans wondering why a player who refused to participate in one of the key skills of the game could be voted Carlisle's best player? Well, the answer lay in his skill when he had the ball on the ground.

First to notice his ability was Manchester City manager Jock Thomson, who signed him for City after one viewing. The two endured a difficult relationship however and in Shankly's first close-season as Carlisle manager, he made a move for the gifted winger.

The board shuddered at the club-record £4,000 fee Shankly offered to pay City, and when he further informed them that he would allow Hogan to remain in Manchester and train with the Maine Road club during the week, before travelling to Carlisle on match days, they thought the world had finally gone mad.

But Shankly knew what he was getting and Hogan didn't disappoint him or the fans that came to idolise him. He made his debut for the team in slightly darker blue shirts in a 1–0 victory over Wrexham on 1 September 1949.

Hogan's forte was to get the ball down, drift inside and out, before setting up the perfect cross or shot. The fans loved him, and he grew to love them. Referring to them and his manager in later life, Hogan commented:

The fans are everything, without them there wouldn't be football. Bill Shankly always said we should always be open and honest with fans. He was right too.

The respect was mutual. Two famous Carlisle managers were fulsome in their praise for Billy Hogan towards the end of their respective careers. Shankly himself wrote:

> When I went to Carlisle, I signed Billy Hogan. The fans up there thought he was Matthews! He was a sensational footballer, one of the best I ever signed or managed and that includes many of these I manage at Liverpool. I would have taken him with me wherever I could but sadly he enjoyed life at Carlisle too much.

One of Shankly's successors in the Blues' hot-seat would prove to be the most successful Carlisle United manager of them all: Alan Ashman. Like Broadis and Shankly, Ashman also played for the club. As a youngster in the early fifties, he had the pleasure of playing with Hogan and his prolific partner Jimmy 'Wham' Whitehouse. In the mid-1970s, with his playing and managerial career behind him, Ashman was still in no doubt about who was the best player he ever saw:

> Billy Hogan was the best footballer I played with during my time at Carlisle. In fact I can't think of anyone at any club I have played for or managed who was more attacking, creative and loyal. I learned a lot from playing alongside Bill and Jimmy Whitehouse. Bill was the complete footballer – he was one of those people who just commanded respect. Players would listen to him when he spoke. If I had Billy Hogan in my First Division team then we wouldn't have been relegated. He was technically the most gifted player I knew.

On the opposite flank, Shankly tried various players after selling the popular Workington lad Lloyd Iceton at the end of the 1949–50 season – a sale designed to balance the books somewhat.

The first player Shankly tried in Iceton's position was Jimmy Kelly, a Tottenham Hotspur reserve who had made the journey north in February 1949. He never broke into the first team at White Hart Lane but initially started his new career well, playing over a dozen games before the end of the season.

But by the start of the new 1950–51season, and following Iceton's departure, Shankly appeared to be having second thoughts about Kelly, whose goal return wasn't coming anywhere near that of the former winger. After scouring the market again for someone similar to the goalscoring outside-left, Shankly masterminded the low-risk signing of a player who fitted the bill perfectly.

Alex McCue, like Tommy Kinloch, followed the Shankly-to-Shankly route in October 1950. McCue was destined to have a brief Carlisle career but was someone who would have a significant role to play in this particular story.

He had been at Falkirk for two seasons but found himself in and out of the side, in fact when he was signed the local press referred to him as a 'Falkirk reserve.' The oddest thing about the signing however, were the terms. The Bairns agreed to United's proposal to pay them no fee unless they retained the player at the end of the season.

Jack Billingham was another Shankly signing. He signed the Burnley veteran (35) on the same day he captured the signature of Billy Hogan. Like Hogan, Waters and some of the others, Billingham, with experience of playing in the First Division would prove to be a useful utility man filling in at both half-back and centre-forward.

And like Hogan (and Phil Turner for that matter), Billingham got his manager's permission to continue to live in Lancashire, where he would train during the week with Burnley before joining his Carlisle teammates on match-days.

Other players in the squad included local lad Geoff Hill, who would wrack up almost two hundred games at full-back by the time his Carlisle career ended in 1958. And the popular North Easterner Dennis Stokoe who wouldn't be far off that figure either.

Stokoe was a defender who could play at full-back or half-back, and distinguished himself for not only Carlisle but Cumbrian neighbours Workington as well. There was a strange symmetry to Stokoe's time in Cumberland as he totted up over a hundred games for the Blues and the Reds, and played under Bill Shankly at both clubs.

Dennis was an out-and-out defender and during his six years in the Blue half of the county, only scored two goals. One of them however, was the club's 1,000th league goal in the 1–1 draw with York City on Boxing Day 1949.

Edgar Duffett from Norwich City and later, Jimmy 'Buster' Brown from Queen of the South were also Shankly acquisitions.

Another essential part of the set up was trainer Fred Ford. Ford was born in Kent in 1916 and started his playing career as an Arsenal trainee. He played for a few London clubs either side of the war before being signed by Ivor Broadis for Carlisle from Milwall in 1947. "Fred was a good bargain," recalls his former manager, "he kept the whole place going after his playing days were over."

What Ivor is referring to is that after Ford's brief playing career at Brunton Park (he only played 28 games over two seasons) he took up a coaching career and became an integral part of the Shankly set-up as the head Trainer. It was at this second career that Ford excelled.

A young local player, Eric Thompson, signed for the club shortly after Shankly left (much to his regret) and remembers Ford (and some of his unorthodox methods) well:

> Fred Ford was a brilliant trainer. They reckon he was one of the top two or three coaches in the UK – he had the same qualifications as Walter Winterbotton. He acted as trainer and what you would now call a physio. When he couldn't fathom a problem with an injury he used to sometimes send players to Geordie Long who worked down at Denton Holme as someone who worked on muscles and bones.

Geordie wasn't registered, so his practice was frowned upon but he was ahead of his time. Between them Fred and Geordie would always get the players ready to play!

Shankly's engrained enthusiasm for the game was infectious and this rubbed off on the whole squad who grew to revere their boss (a trait that was to follow him wherever he went). He called everybody 'son' (apart from Jackie 'Hector' Lindsay!) which was invariably pronounced '*san*' with his Ayrshire brogue.

He insisted on his players always eating well, despite the rationing that still gripped the country. He particularly liked the players to eat eggs and knew a local farmer who brought in a few dozen eggs and some butter before each weekend. It was Fred Ford's job to count out the eggs and cut the butter into the appropriate number of chunks and put the packages in a cubby hole beside the dressing room.

Having more players than eggs and butter, Shankly got into the routine of ensuring the players who were playing on the Saturday were the ones to get a package of eggs and butter the day before the game. It became the tell-tale signal for the boss' team selection the following day. Fred Ford later told a story about one Friday morning when he saw Dennis Stokoe peeking into the cubby hole. "Sorry Dennis," said Fred, "no eggs for you this week!"

Previous page: The opening day team for the 1950–51 season.

Back row left to right: Jack Billingham, Alex McIntosh, Geoff Twenty-man, Jim MacLaren, Bill Caton, Dennis Stokoe. Front row: Billy Hogan, Phil Turner, Jimmy Jackson, George Dick, Jimmy Kelly.

The team on the field at Highbury before the Arsenal game

Back row left to right: Norman Coupe, Alex McIntosh, Jim MacLaren, Tommy Kinloch, Geoff Twentyman, Paddy Waters. Front row: Billy Hogan, Phil Turner, Jack Billingham, Jimmy Jackson, Alex McCue

The one time Shankly fell out with his players – and everybody else for that matter – is when his team lost. Finding any excuse to blame anyone (or any*thing*) for a defeat, two priceless anecdotes, originating from his players, sum the manager up (and demonstrate the players' mischievous affection for him).

The first involved Geoff Twentyman, who loved reciting the tale of a half-time bollocking he received from Shankly, amid howls of laughter.

Shankly made him skipper upon his arrival at Brunton Park and saw him as the fulcrum of the side. In one game, when the team had played particularly poorly and found themselves 2–0 down at half time, Shankly – knowing his team had lost the pre-game coin toss – rounded on his captain in the dressing room:

"Geoff, what did you call in the toss-up?"

"I called heads boss," replied the skipper.

"Jesus, *san*!" cried the angry Shankly in all seriousness, "*why didn't ye call tails?!*"

The other tale involved the two Jacks: Billingham and Lindsay.

If they won a game, Shankly's team didn't have to train on the following Monday, as a reward for their hard work. If they lost, they were always in on the Monday; but if they drew a game they were never sure – it all depended on how they played. If Shankly spoke to them, it meant he was reasonably pleased with their effort and they would be excused training as a result; but if he ignored them and didn't speak at all (something that happened every time they put in a poor performance) they knew they had to train.

After one particular drawn game, the players were unsure what the result meant as far as training on Monday was concerned. Billingham and Lindsay were in the dressing room and the boss was nowhere to be seen.

Billingham turns to Lindsay and asks, "So are we training or what?"

Lindsay replies, "It looks like it, because Hector hasn't spoke to us."

Billingham decides to go in search of the manager. He comes back into the dressing room a few minutes later full of enthusiasm, "Hey Jackie, we don't have to train on Monday!"

"How do you know?"

"The boss just spoke to me!"

"What did he say?"

"He told me to fuck off!"

A Good Cup Run

The classic aspirational phrase of every lower league club.

Carlisle United's cup run of 1950–51 lasted a relatively modest four games, but those games were packed with so many incidents and stories that they have since overshadowed the whole of what was the club's most successful ever League campaign.

Bill Shankly's first full season in charge saw the Blues finish a creditable ninth in Division Three North – a run which included a ten-game unbeaten run at home between January and the end of the campaign. But he was about to experience his first taste of off-field politics that would constantly frustrate him throughout his managerial career.

In June 1950, at the Annual General Meeting, the shareholders association expressed their concern about the finances for the club. There were rumblings about the quality of the players and the fact that Shankly had spent big in his 18 months at the club (admittedly his outlay included the £18,000 received for Ivor Broadis). The chairman of the association asked for a comment on the future of the club and progress on the transfer system.

Shankly tried to assure the association that he was working to build a better squad for the future. He told the meeting, "I'm glad we did not get promoted because we are not ready. But I believe we have a better chance next season and that is our stated aim."

The truth was, winning promotion for the first time in the club's history was going to be a big ask; Shankly still hadn't settled on his preferred squad and he knew that he had to be seen to be balancing the books with good sales as well as good buys.

During that close season in came wing-half Tommy Kinloch from Falkirk, and inside-forwards Jimmy Jackson and Edgar Duffett from Bolton Wanderers and Norwich City respectively. Out went Lloyd Iceton to Tranmere Rovers, Ken Walshaw to Bradford City and Terry Seed to Accrington.

Such was the dilemma of the lower league manager: buying and selling to both placate the board on the one hand, while satisfying the fans with good performances on the other. Whatever he decides, he leaves himself open to criticism. The sale of Iceton in particular was a case in point: the move boosted the club's coffers but proved unpopular with the supporters, as was reflected in the *Carlisle Journal*:

> Likeable Lloyd Leaves!
> We will no longer see our Workington lad rattle the rigging with one of his left foot thunderbolts. He will be greatly missed as a United player. A great wit and a songster he would always lead the singing on the bus on the way home. This natural left footer and most likeable of lads has left us. We can only wish him well at Tranmere.

And things didn't get much better when the season got underway. Stated intentions are one thing but when the first game ended in a 1-0 defeat at Southport, fans could have been forgiven for thinking they were in for nothing more than another steady, mid-table campaign. Little did they know at this point that the opening day defeat would in fact be the last time Carlisle would fail to score until the following January.

The first home game set the tone for the free-scoring season ahead with a 3–0 win over Gateshead. The team quickly set the tone with their slick movement and goal-hungry approach when in possession.

Free scoring arguably became hare-em scare-em as the Blues set about slugging it out with their various third tier opponents. A week after the home game with Gateshead, the reverse fixture at Redheugh Park was lost by the odd goal in seven. By the time Mansfield defeated United at the end of September Carlisle had won six and lost four of their 11 games which had delivered 33 goals; the wins included victories over Scunthorpe United, one of the two new teams added to the league and big spending Bradford Park Avenue who had just dropped down from Division Two.

If their offensive play gave cause for some optimism, their defensive play caused concern in equal amount due to the inability to find the right-half-back combination.

The Mansfield game was significant as it was to prove the last game of the prolific and popular forward George Dick.

League *or* Cup glory seemed a long way off as the *Carlisle Journal* asked where the club was going. After the team's home draw with bottom club Shrewsbury in mid-October under the headline, 'Theme song for the United supporters' the piece suggested:

> Frank Sinatra would stir a responsive chord in the breast of every supporter of Carlisle United if he came to Her Majesty's Theatre this week and sang his plaintive refrain '*Bewitched, Bothered and Bewildered*'. Supporters are certainly bothered that their much experimented team is still only in the experimental stage – and the cup ties barely a month distant.

In particular, the local press reflected the fans' dismay at the sale of Dick, labelling it '...thoroughly bad business.' It came about when Stockport County's manager Andy Beattie noticed that Dick had been left out of the team to play Shrewsbury and contacted Shankly to enquire about the centre-forward's possible availability. The striker met with his manager to express his dissatisfaction at being selected for the reserves and at the meeting Shankly informed Dick of Beattie's approach.

Dick immediately expressed his interest in the move and within twenty four hours, was in Preston discussing personal terms with the Stockport manager. Bradford City tried to usurp the deal at the last minute and came in with a bigger offer, but Dick was happy with Beattie's sales pitch and decided to move to Edgeley Park.

The local press and supporters may well have been disgruntled by the sale but no one was more frustrated than Shankly himself, who understood the need to balance the books. With the solid performances of Lindsay, Caton and Turner, and the development of Jackson, Shankly recognised that the return of nearly £3,000 for the ageing (if still highly rated) forward was good business.

The other frustration for Shankly and the home fans was that first choice left-back Alec Scott suffered an injury during the Shrewsbury game that would certainly keep him sidelined for several weeks. (Dick and Scott were the two former Cup Finalists from Blackpool and Leicester respectively). It was unfortunate for the team as Scott had played superbly since his arrival half way through the previous season. His absence would mean another chance for the local squad man Norman Coupe.

As Dick went out, two new forward players came into the squad. Jimmy 'Buster' Brown came across the border from Queen of the South; the rather mis-named Buster would prove himself to be quite a clever ball player, specialising in deft flicks and back-heels to bring his fellow forwards into play.

The other signing was classic Carlisle United. Shankly went to his brother Bob at Falkirk and negotiated the acquisition of reserve winger Alex McCue. The deal was that Carlisle paid no transfer fee for the winger unless they decided to retain his services at the end of the season. It seemed a particularly good deal when McCue scored on his debut against high flying Bradford City in a 4–2 win; he then followed it up with two more the following week in a 4–0 drubbing of Rochdale.

Whether by accident or design, the Blues were now settling into a consistent run (that would ultimately see them go unbeaten for fifteen games) but Shankly still had concerns about his back line. Although Geoff Twentyman was looking accomplished at centre-half, the manager was still unsure about the half-backs where the ever willing utility men Jack Billingham and Spud Hayton were doing enough to keep the summer signing Tommy Kinloch out of the team.

With this potentially problematic position in mind, Shankly spent most of November 1950 tracking two Manchester City players he believed would complement the outstanding Twentyman. Billy Walsh and Albert Emptage were both understudies at the Maine Road club but that didn't stop them racking up over one hundred games each for the Sky Blues. Shankly was confident he could persuade them to make the step down where they would get regular first team football at a club pushing for promotion to the Second Division. The problem was, City were in no mood to lower their asking price of £5,500 for Walsh and £3,500 for Emptage and the Carlisle board were not prepared to match their valuations of the players.

(November also saw the death of Shankly's uncle, director Billy Blyth. Blyth's association with the club dated back to 1905.)

With no new recruits on board therefore, it was Billingham and Hayton again who lined up alongside Twentyman for the FA Cup first round – a home tie against Barrow on 25 November 1950.

What made the tie even more worrying was the fact that it became known that the Liverpool chief scout had travelled to Brunton Park to see the highly rated Geoff Twentyman who was fast making a name for himself. The Merseyside representative took his place amongst 17,000 spectators.

As is usual in cup football, the game bore little resemblance to the two teams' respective League positions. Among the Barrow number were former Carlisle players Billy Buchanan (full-back) and Billy Gordon (centre-forward). Despite their former club starting quite brightly, it was the Holker Street outfit who gradually seized the initiative and after twenty minutes they found themselves well on top.

Norman Coupe had performed particularly well in his first game deputising for the injured Scott (the excellent 4–2 win at Bradford a month earlier) which had led to a confident, competent run in the team. He now found himself second best to Billy Rogers, the Barrow outside-right however. Rogers was the main supply line to Gordon and George King in the middle and between them, they were giving the United defence plenty to worry about.

Against the run of play it was the home side who took the lead. The ball was slicked through midfield before each of the forward line of Bill Caton, Buster Brown and Phil Turner were all involved to set up the wing man Alex McCue – who was already developing a good habit of joining in from the left – to net his fourth goal in only his sixth start.

The goal wasn't enough to wrestle the initiative from Barrow however, as they came back into the game immediately. Their efforts were rewarded before half-time when Rogers again created down the right hand side and Gordon slotted the equaliser in from close range. United were fortunate to be level at the break and the home fans were hopeful that some of the half time Shankly magic would change the tone in the second period.

It didn't quite work out that way when Rogers again caused problems for Coupe down the Barrow right and the full-back brought him down to concede a penalty barely five minutes into the second period. As the crowd hushed, centre-forward Gordon ran up to take the kick; Jim MacLaren moved to his right but managed to stick out on ungainly leg to block the powerful shot that was aimed straight down the middle. Coupe redeemed himself by racing in and clearing the rebound to safety.

Before anyone could talk about 'turning points' Carlisle suffered another setback when minutes later, stand-in half-back Jack Billingham came off second best against the tough Barrow centre-forward and collapsed with a badly twisted knee. Fred Ford raced on with the magic sponge but it was all Billingham could do to put any weight on his right side.

In these pre-substitute days, Shankly was forced to reorganise his side; he moved Bill Caton to half-back, switched Alex McCue to a more central position and put the 'passenger' Billingham out wide on the left.

Barrow saw their chance to press home their advantage and mounted a concerted effort. For fifteen minutes, the re-shaped Carlisle rear-guard weathered the storm before a clearance saw Buster Brown and Phil Turner race up-field; a slick interchange between the two resulted in the clinical Turner making no mistake. Somewhat unjustly, Carlisle hung on for an unlikely win.

The draw for the next round was made and the Blues were pulled out to play either Lincoln or Southport away from home on 9 December. One local reporter pulled no punches in his summary of the Barrow game:

> United played just about their worst game of the season, and if this is their cup-tie form, they stand in need of strengthening in nearly every department.

The problem was – as far as the cup was concerned – the deadline for signing new players for the next round passed on the same day as the first round games. That notwithstanding, with Billingham's injury (diagnosed after the Barrow game as a knee ligament injury) and Kinloch still untried, Shankly stepped up his chase for a half-back, knowing that his team had built up a head of steam to this point and it was important to keep the momentum going.

Frustrated at his lack of success at trying to prise away Walsh and Emptage from Manchester City, it was at this point that he turned his attention to his old team mate Paddy Waters at Preston. Despite Waters' reservations on his arrival at Brunton Park, it proved a match made in heaven, with Waters settling into his new surroundings and the home fans taking to the hard-tackling former Irish International in a heart-beat.

Confident in the abilities of Waters and Twentyman, and with Billingham's injury, Shankly called up his summer recruit Tommy Kinloch to form a new look back line. Waters and Kinloch travelled down to Manchester with the team prior to them making their debuts for the club at Stockport County the following day. The presence of the new recruits was not the only noteworthy point regarding this particular weekend.

In the same hotel as Carlisle was none other than the Arsenal team who were playing at Bolton on the same day that the Blues were due to meet Stockport. Shankly inevitably sought out his fellow manager and engaged in conversation with Tom Whittaker. Carlisle were due to play Southport in the second round of the cup the following week, and as the two shook hands at the end of their chat, Shankly told his opposite number that he expected to beat the Lancashire club and said he hoped to meet up with Whittaker and Arsenal in the next round! (Shankly, director Billy Little and Secretary Bill Clarke had all travelled to Haig Avenue to see Southport beat Lincoln 3-2 in their first round replay.)

The game against Stockport itself was also noteworthy as Waters and Kinloch came up against the former Carlisle favourite George Dick who led the County attack. The debutants performed well and goals from Jackie Lindsay and yet another from Alex McCue secured a good away victory.

Buoyed by their team's ever improving League form, the fans responded to the away Cup tie at Southport with great enthusiasm. Demand for tickets was high and five special trains were laid on by British Railways to take an estimated 2,200 Cumbrians to the Lancashire coast.

With Paddy Waters ineligible, Spud Hayton was brought back in to the rear guard alongside Twentyman and Kinloch, while Jackie Lindsay replaced Buster Brown up front.

A classic end-to-end cup tie ensued, as is usually the case when both sides seemed relieved of any League caginess. Early efforts came and went in both goalmouths before Southport settled in to a deep line that stepped out in unison to catch the Carlisle forwards offside (quite unusual for the day); Lindsay, Turner and Hogan were all caught in the trap before ten minutes had passed. McCue then set up the visitors' best chance when he dribbled down the left before cutting the ball back; onrushing was the unlikely figure of Tommy Kinloch whose 'defender's effort' went high over the bar.

At the other end, a sliding tackle by the skipper McIntosh halted the Southport centre-forward as he threatened MacLaren's goal.

The breakthrough came just before the quarter hour: Bill Caton won possession just beyond halfway; he carried it forward ten yards and played a slide-rule pass through to Jackie Lindsay, who this time, timed his run perfectly and slammed that ball into the bottom corner without breaking stride.

From the re-start, the home side countered and forced a sharp save from MacLaren who had to turn the ball away for a corner. The corner itself was cleared but as it was met by Bill Caton on the halfway line, the inside-forward's studs caught in the heavy ground and he collapsed to the floor holding his knee. Fred Ford ran on the field but Caton discovered that the trainer's magic sponge was not that magic after all and he had to be carried from the field by Ford and Geoff Twentyman.

For the second tie in succession the Blues were handicapped by the loss of a player. Despite this, the imbalance wasn't terribly evident as the visitors won a free kick on the edge of the Southport box, the home side meanwhile countered with three corners in quick succession. With five minutes to go to the break, Phil Turner received the ball half way inside the opposition half; he turned and set off at pace, taking out two defenders in the process; as the Southport 'keeper Anderson advanced, Turner ripped in a shot before he could set himself, and the ten men of Carlisle found themselves two-up going into half-time.

News reached the press box during the interval that Caton's injury was knee ligaments; much to everyone's surprise he gamely limped onto the field with his teammates for the second half but was so incapacitated that he had to be helped off again before the game resumed.

No sooner was the game back underway that ten men almost became nine: Alex McCue was flattened as he challenged for a ball down the inside left channel vacated by Caton. With one wing man back on his feet, the other started to control possession for the visitors: Billy Hogan was at his brilliant best for the first fifteen minutes of the half, with his mazy runs and incisive passing.

It was on the hour that Hogan outpaced his full-back and crossed a low ball into the middle; Lindsay darted towards the near post taking two defenders with him but cleverly stepped over the ball creating space for the unmarked Turner behind him to smash in his second of the game.

If Carlisle's performance against Barrow was ropy, this performance against Southport was outstanding. Playing with ten men for seventy-five minutes, it was only in the last ten that the home side pulled one back and pressured their tiring opponents in the final minutes; but to no avail.

Shankly was typically fulsome in his praise of his charges and their 3–1 victory:

> The boys were magnificent today. There's not a team in this division who can live with us when we play like that. To lose Bill Caton so early was a blow but you would never know it, we dominated them.

If the supporters thought things couldn't get any better after one of the Blues' best displays of the season, it was just about to: 'United receive the plumb draw!' cried the *Evening News* on 11 December. 'Carlisle are drawn to meet the mighty Arsenal at Highbury in the third round of the FA Cup.'

The piece went on to extol the virtues of the biggest club in the land with their six league titles and the fact that they were the reigning cup holders. None of this phased Shankly of course whose team were unbeaten since 30 September:

> It is a wonderful draw and we are full of confidence. I don't want to make predictions but we will go down to London and play the same level of football we do here at Brunton Park, and we will do our best to entertain the Arsenal supporters. Arsenal's tactics will not be new to me. I played six months for them as a guest during the war and know most of their tricks. It is a big team against a small one but we are hopeful.

Arsenal manager Tom Whittaker gave his response to the draw:

> We are grateful for a home draw and look forward again to meet Bill Shankly the Carlisle manager who played for us during the war.

Shankly focused his players' minds on the task at hand between the draw and the game; Carlisle were near the top of the Division and promotion looked a real possibility for the first time in the club's history. He was aware that the cup could easily become a distraction and destabilise the solid campaign.

In a strange quirk of the fixture list, Carlisle met Southport again the following week, this time at Brunton Park. Back in the Carlisle side for his home debut was Paddy Waters (replacing Spud Hayton) and Edgar Duffet made a rare start in place of the injured Bill Caton who was obviously going to be missing for some weeks – a period that would almost certainly include the big game.

But back to the Southport match: different competition, different teams, different venue, same result – Carlisle again ran out 3–1 winners to keep their impressive promotion push going (two from Lindsay and another from

Alex McCue). The Blues were again outstanding on the day with Waters particularly catching the eye. The one player who had a quiet game was Duffet and while he was struggling, Jimmy Jackson was scoring a hat-trick for the reserves in the North Eastern League Cup against Annfield Plain. It was a performance that would get Jackson back in the first team where he was destined to remain for most of the season.

Off the field meanwhile, attention was already turning to the big cup tie when details of tickets were released on 13 December. It was noted that tickets were over-subscribed in London as soon as the sale was announced. As far as the away quota was concerned, normal communication links were not trusted for the precious cargo, so a special train was commissioned to transport them to Crewe, where they were met by a Carlisle messenger.

With prices at 7s and 10s 6d applications were invited in writing to the secretary at Brunton Park no later than 20 December.

After the appropriate badgering from his son, Claude Daley was one of five thousand applications. As each letter applied for more than one ticket, there were many who were going to be disappointed.

Back on the field – in a hectic end to the year – United played a further four games, winning three and drawing one. Their 1–0 win over Bradford Park Avenue was their eighth win in a run of 13 games undefeated. The big worry however was that defensive linchpin Geoff Twentyman was a major doubt for the big game after receiving a muscle strain against Accrington Stanley on Christmas Day. But following the holiday period, the Blues were lying second in the table behind Rotherham, with just one game to play before the big one against Arsenal.

The game in question was another game against Barrow at Brunton Park. Whether the Ziggers had revenge on their mind for their unjust defeat in the cup, or whether jealousy took over knowing that their rivals were about to make the trip of a footballing lifetime, the game descended into a bruising affair. The score (1–1) was almost incidental as Carlisle counted the cost in terms of injuries: each of the wing-halves Kinloch and Waters had received knocks while centre-forward Jackie Lindsay had to leave the field with a mouth injury after a collision with the centre-half.

Jackie Lindsay in scoring action against Darlington in 1950

It was reported afterward that he would need to visit the dentist to have a molar looked at, but when he did so, the news broke on the Monday afternoon that Lindsay had actually fractured his jaw in the challenge. First-choice centre-forward Jackie Lindsay was out of the Arsenal game.

Years later, Lindsay told his son John what had actually happened that day:

> Before the game their big centre-half came up to me a said, "I'm going to break your fucking jaw!" I told him to fuck off because I used to get that sort of thing every week. But that's what he did. I went up for a high ball and I could just see the elbow coming and bang! I broke my leg twice during my career but nothing hurt like that – it was ten times worse.

John concluded that his dad had to eat through a straw for weeks afterward. (An insight into the sacrifices footballers of the day had to make comes when John also told me that his dad had all his teeth taken out deliberately before his career really began. "My mam said he had a lovely set of teeth and he had them all taken out because he knew what was coming.")

Hiding his obvious disappointment at the loss of his main striker, Shankly was in bullish mood in the days before the game. He informed the press that there would be no special training in preparation for the big game, and when pressed about the feeling in the camp in light of the opposition, he famously replied, "Arsenal, who are they? Never heard of them!"

Arsenal, Who Are They?

So what *was* all the fuss about? Well, there were several reasons.

The people of Carlisle were no different from any others in austere post-war Britain: desperate for something that would break the monotonous ration-dominated recovery that was now dragging on as long as the war itself.

Whereas some today might assume that football would be a trivial insignificance by comparison to the hardship of everyday life, in actual fact the opposite was true. There was little else to do: the dance on a Saturday night if you could afford; the pictures; and then (mainly for the male population) the match on a Saturday or Thursday afternoon.

In an effort to excite and inspire the populous into creating a community based club therefore, Shankly to a certain degree was pushing at an open door.

The other factor was the FA Cup itself – although a team like Carlisle United could never come close to winning the trophy, it cannot be overstated how big the Cup was. There were no European competitions and no League Cup; ostensibly there were only two major competitions, the League Championship and the FA Cup, and one was as big as the other.

The major difference the Cup had over the League, of course, was its romance, and the opportunity for minnows to play against the great and the good of the English game. And there was none bigger or better than Arsenal.

Matt Busby had not yet begun to mould Manchester United into the nation's favourite team, and obviously, it would be over a decade before Bill

Shankly would set about surpassing United's achievements with Liverpool. In fact to put Arsenal's stature in to some context, in 1950 their combined League and Cup successes surpassed both Manchester clubs and Liverpool put together. As for their modern-day London rivals, Chelsea had never won either the League or the Cup, while Tottenham only had two FA Cup victories on their honours board. (Other clubs like Wolverhampton Wanderers and Portsmouth would enjoy post-war success but that was ahead of this story too.)

Arsenal on the other hand, had six League Championships (and two runners' up) and three FA Cups (and three runners' up) by the time the draw was made for the 1950–51 season.

Not only were they the biggest team in England, they were considered the biggest club side in Europe. Many Continental leagues were still in their infancy; the exceptions being in Italy and Spain. Spanish giants Real Madrid and Barcelona had only six domestic titles between them (again it would be a few years before Madrid would dominate Europe. Today the two giants have over fifty titles between them). The Turin giants, Juventus and Torino were probably the only clubs who could claim to match Arsenal in terms of stature and success: Juventus had eight titles and two cup victories, while their neighbours had six titles and two cups.

Arsenal began life in late 1886 when fifteen football-mad munitions workers from the Dial Square workshop at the Woolwich Arsenal formed a team with a dream of playing in the Football League. On Christmas Day 1886 they changed their name to Royal Arsenal.

'Woolwich' Arsenal was adopted in 1891, two years before it was elected to the Football League.

With modest finances, success, and frankly, interest in Woolwich, the club was taken over in 1910 by Fulham Chairman and entrepreneur Henry Norris. Norris decided to move his new club north of the river to one of the more populated areas of the city in an effort to lurch it forward: more interest equalled bigger crowds, which meant more money and with it greater success on and off the field.

In 1913 the Woolwich club moved to Highbury in North London and ditched its Christian name in the process. Re-located and re-branded, Arsenal were born. Not that it made much difference; within the year the country was at war and first-class football effectively ceased to exist.

Norris kept his powder dry until the war's conclusion and then set about engineering his club into the top Division, despite the fact that Arsenal finished only fifth in the 1914–15 season!

While the war was on, Norris had gained a knighthood and become an MP, and appeared to use all of his influence and expertise in talking his club up, figuratively and literally.

In 1919 it was decided by the League to increase the number of clubs in the First Division from 20 to 22 and Sir Henry somehow convinced the other chairmen at the AGM to elect Arsenal to the top flight along with Derby and Preston (who finished first and second). This meant that Barnsley and Wolves (who finished third and fourth in Second Division) were overlooked, and, incredibly, a team was relegated from the First Division to make way for Norris's team. It gets worse – that team was none other than Tottenham Hotspur! (Arsenal have been a top flight team ever since, without technically ever having won promotion!)

Norris had achieved his dream of seeing Arsenal in the top flight but modest performances in their first five years (never finishing in the top half of the Division) suggested further change was needed. That change came in 1925.

In an earlier chapter, I suggested that Bill Shankly would be viewed by many football historians as being in the top handful of managers of all time. The man who became Arsenal manager in 1925 would be viewed by some of that number as being *the* greatest of them all.

Like Shankly, Herbert Chapman was born in a small mining village [in his case] in Yorkshire in 1878. As well as being a keen sportsman, Herbert was a bright lad who gravitated to the Sheffield Technical College, where he studied engineering.

He travelled the country taking engineering jobs and playing football as an amateur for a whole host of clubs as diverse as Stalybridge Rovers and Tottenham Hotspur. But it was in football management that his genius manifested itself.

Chapman became manager of Northampton Town of the Southern League in 1907 – they were Champions the following season. This led to a job back in Yorkshire with Second Division Leeds City, before the Great War broke out, and then a move across to Huddersfield Town as peace returned.

Within three years Huddersfield were First Division Champions; another Championship followed in 1924–25 and the hat-trick would be achieved the following season.

But Chapman was not around to celebrate this third title; Sir Henry Norris recognised him as the best manager in the League and moved to take him south to Highbury by offering him £2,000 a year salary. Chapman already dominated the national game with the Yorkshire club and quickly recognised the even greater opportunity with the untapped potential Arsenal afforded. It was almost one of his first actions that set the scene for the decades of dominance that was to follow.

By coincidence, at the same time Chapman moved to Arsenal, the Football Association changed the offside rule; they decreed that instead of requiring three defending players between an attacker and the goalline when the ball was played forward, that number should be reduced to two. The innovative Chapman changed the system of his team therefore to take full advantage of the new rules. He introduced a formation that would become known as the 'WM', with one of the inside-forwards dropping back to act as a link between defence and attack.

The 'playmaker' was born. But the first exponent of the role is unlikely to be mentioned in the same breath as Cruyff, Zidane or Messi (*other than here of course!*).

Andy Neil played a modest 57 games for Arsenal and when Chapman arrived, he was a veteran playing in the third team at Highbury. His new manager took one look at him and described him as being "…as slow as a funeral but has ball control and can pass the ball accurately." He therefore put him into the heart of his team, and the move the paid instant dividends.

From nowhere, Chapman guided his new team to the runners' up spot behind his old team Huddersfield in 1925–26 (Arsenal had narrowly avoided relegation in 1925). The following season, Arsenal reached their first FA Cup Final (losing to Cardiff City) before returning to Wembley three years later.

The FA Cup Final of 1930 would be a showdown between 'Chapman's two clubs' Arsenal and Huddersfield Town; it would prove a watershed moment in the history of Arsenal Football Club and signalled a changing of the guard at the summit of the English game. The Gunners won the game 2–0 and achieved their first major honour.

Their first League Championship followed a year later. The visionary manager was changing his club and the game forever.

Chapman continually altered playing formations and tactics on the field that the opposition couldn't live with (tactics they were all soon to copy). He added the famous white sleeves to his team's red shirts and gave them hooped socks to make them stand out both to spectators and to each other during the game, and advocated the introduction of numbers for the same reason. (*As a player himself – as early as 1910 – he painted his own boots yellow for the same reason!*)

His ambition for his club was reflected in the transfer market as he set about signing good players and turning them into great players, such as David Jack, Alex James and Eddie Hapgood.

(If Andy Neil didn't go down in the annals of great playmakers, then Alex James certainly did. Already on the CV of 'wee Alex' was his orchestrating of the 1928 'Wembley Wizards' 5–1 demolition of England. He transferred from Preston to Arsenal a year later and assumed the role of midfield genius in Chapman's team).

Another Chapman signing was Cliff Bastin, who wrote about his old boss in 1950:

> There was an aura of greatness about him. He possessed a cheery self-confidence. His power of inspiration and gift of foresight were his greatest attributes. I think his qualities were worthy of an even

better reward. He should have been Prime Minister, and might have but for the lack of opportunities entailed by his position in the social scale.

(This could be one of the Liverpool players of the early 1970s writing about Shankly).

Off the field Chapman was equally active. He lobbied the authorities to introduce floodlights, and set about building the stadium thousands of Carlisle United fans were to marvel at twenty years later.

And it didn't stop with the stadium either: in an audacious bid to publicise his club nationally and globally, he convinced the London Electric Railway to change of the name of its Gillespie Road tube station, just around the corner from the ground. "Whoever heard of Gillespie Road?" he asked, "It is Arsenal around here."

Tom Whittaker (left), Alex James and Herbert Chapman on the bench during the 1932 Cup Final (James was injured and couldn't play in the match)

On 5 November 1932, Arsenal became a fixture on maps throughout London. (The naming ceremony was carried out by the Fifth Earl of Lonsdale, Hugh Lowther, who was a director of Arsenal at the time.)

Bernard Joy, player, historian, writer, said of Chapman:

> There are two kinds of visionary; those that dream of a whole new world and those who dream of just one thing. Chapman's vision was of the greatest football team in the world. His genius was in actually creating something close to that.

(Again, remind you of anyone?)

Chapman's men were within a couple of games of achieving the century's first elusive League and Cup double in 1932 but finished runners' up in both (to Everton and Newcastle respectively). They bounced back in 1933 however with their second title in three years. At this rate Chapman was on course to repeat his engineering of Huddersfield's hat-trick during the Twenties.

The feat was duly achieved by the club with League Championships in 1934 and 1935. But, like at Huddersfield, Chapman wasn't around to see the triumph. Tragically, he caught a cold on New Year's Day 1934 which developed into pneumonia. Chapman died within a week.

The football nation was shocked at the news of the passing of the most successful manager of the modern era.

His legacy was the continued success of his club: director George Allison became Managing Director, while 'backroom staff' Joe Shaw, John Peters and Tom Whittaker concentrated on the day-to-day running of the club. The players themselves took extra responsibilities and the club marched on after the great man's passing as though nothing had ever happened.

By the end of the decade, the club that Chapman built was a dynasty of triumph with five League Championships (1931, 1933, 1934, 1935 and 1938) and two FA Cup victories (1930 and 1936). Had competitive European football been in existence in the 1930s, it is no exaggeration to suggest

Arsenal would have probably added two or three European Cups to that role of honour.

We will never know, of course, but the circumstantial evidence for this suggestion is almost overwhelming: not only did the club play, and defeat, foreign opposition on a fairly regular basis during this period, but Arsenal players won no fewer than 140 caps for their respective British Isles' teams. Notable among these fixtures was a 3–2 England victory over Italy in 1934 – the England team contained *seven* Arsenal players.

The art deco facade of Arsenal Stadium in 1950

And the marble-halled interior with bust of Herbert Chapman

Allison completed the stadium which Chapman had started with the art-deco East Stand that matched its twin opposite for opulence and grace. Comfortable seating for four thousand spectators, whilst underneath, the players' changing rooms were the height of luxury with heated tiled floors, mechanical and electrical equipment to help fitness and treat injury, and large baths and relaxation areas.

Bill Shankly locked horns with Arsenal's dream team in his Preston days and couldn't hide his admiration writing later:

> My first season in the First Division with Preston was Alex James's last [with Arsenal]. He was a genius. Arsenal were the first team to be really organised and it was a nightmare playing against them. James, Drake, Cliff Bastin, Joe Hulme – what a team that was!

But by the end of the footballing decade, dominated by the club, there was only one blot on the Arsenal record – something that would give Shankly's charges hope some years later.

In 1933 – with Chapman at the helm – Walsall caused a national sensation by dumping Arsenal out of the FA Cup at the third round stage. The Arsenal side had been ravaged by influenza but there was nothing to suggest anything other than a routine victory after Arsenal scouts had watched Walsall draw three and suffer a 5–0 drubbing in the lead up to the big game.

Because of the absenteeism, Chapman played a number of reserves, confident that they were probably more suited to dealing with the tough-tackling lower league team than his absent internationals. Among their number were left-back Tommy Black and centre-forward Charlie Walsh – two names that were to become infamous in Arsenal's history.

In the dressing room before the game, the players' nervousness became evident when Chapman said to Walsh, "I'm expecting a big game from you today son, we're relying on you to show us your best." "Okay, Mr Chapman, I'm ready to play the game of my life," replied Walsh. "Good lad, you'll do," said Chapman looking down at the player's feet, "Oh and by the way, you'd better put your socks on or the crowd will laugh at you!"

It proved a bad omen as Walsall proceeded to hustle and harry their illustrious opponents who couldn't settle into the game. Despite this, the best chance of the first half fell to the hapless Walsh who – now complete with boots *and* socks – missed a virtual open goal.

As Arsenal failed to get their slick passing game going on the muddy surface, Walsall gradually grew in confidence. After sixty minutes, Gilbert Alsop, the home side's centre-forward headed home a Lee corner to put them one up. He recalled: "We had a corner and their full-back Black was marking me. He didn't get up. That was just a big plum pudding that day and I headed it off my forehead straight into the top of the net. I'd been watching Dixie Dean play for England."

He also remembers the foul five minutes later which sealed the game for Walsall. Black's violent lunge at his knee conceded a penalty from which Billy Sheppard scored.

The 2–0 defeat made headline news. Chapman was furious; he refused to allow Tommy Black to return to Highbury and sold him to Portsmouth before the following week was out. Walsh lasted a couple of weeks longer but was transferred to Brentford before the month was out. The Walsall debacle proved to be Black's and Walsh's one and only appearance for the club.

Losing was not something Arsenal were used to throughout the 1930s but as the decade drew to a close, the nation was at war again and (as detailed earlier), competitive League football was suspended as young men from all walks of life were called up to serve King and Country.

Arsenal was representative of football's contribution with forty-two of their forty-four professionals enlisting into the services by September 1939. Five of them never survived the conflict, while several others were wounded, disabled or simply too old to pick up where they'd left off.

Following the war, football clubs had to re-build their playing staff but at sixty-three, Arsenal manager George Allison's appetite for the job was waning. After one post-war season he announced his retirement – the manager's job was taken on by Tom Whittaker.

Like Allison, Whittaker was an Arsenal man through and through. Like his illustrious two predecessors, he was a northerner (Whittaker was a Geordie, while Chapman and Allison were both Yorkshiremen by birth). His connection with the Londoners however dated back to 1920 when he signed professional forms with the Highbury club.

Similarities to Chapman didn't just end with geography either; like the great man, Whittaker had an engineering background; and like Chapman, he was a good all-round sportsman. He graduated to the first team and then to representative honours before Chapman's arrival at the club. But Whittaker had the misfortune of breaking a knee cap in (of all places) Wollongong, near Sydney, Australia while part of an FA Invitational Team in 1925. His playing days were virtually over.

His return to the club coincided with Chapman's appointment in 1925 later that year – the two hit it off immediately and Whittaker found himself re-employed as trainer, a role he also later carried out for the national team.

Whittaker's prowess as a trainer/physio became legendary throughout the sporting world. One of the early non-footballers to visit Highbury was the great Fred Perry who visited Whittaker in the spring of 1936. With a little treatment, help and encouragement – which included training with the first team – Perry re-found his fitness and self-belief and duly won the Wimbledon singles title that summer. Such was Perry's respect for Whittaker that he asked him to train the (ultimately triumphant) British Davis Cup team of Perry, Bunny Austin, Patrick Hughes and Raymond Tuckey.

A parade of sports stars followed Perry through the marble halls to seeing 'the man with the magic hands': cricketers Douglas Jardine, Gubby Allen and Jack Hobbs; world boxing champion Petey Sarron; (and later) golfer Dai Rees, as well as a host of rugby and hockey players.

Like so many of that era, Whittaker was a modest man. Having served briefly in the army at the end of the Great War, he spent most of the 1939–45 conflict in the RAF and was awarded an MBE in the 1945 New Year's Honours List for his secret work in connection with the D-Day landings.

Manager Tom Whittaker with a couple of his players in the palatial Highbury dressing rooms

The war had created a level playing field as far as football was concerned; whereas Arsenal were all-dominant *before* the war, the toll of the conflict and the passing of time had dampened their ardour somewhat, and the question hung around, could they be as successful *after* it?

As the first modern-day super club, Arsenal were by now a national institution, with an aristocratic heritage that was the envy of all others. But like every other club, theirs was a team now in transition, with its mix of pre-war stalwarts – many of whom were now in the autumn of their playing careers – and young up-and-coming players.

The signs were not good for Whittaker as he took the helm. The first post-war season had not gone well. In the first match of the 1946–47 season, Arsenal were hammered 6–1 by Wolves; they proceeded to stumble through the campaign finishing a modest 13th place in the League and a third round exit in the FA Cup to Chelsea. It's clear much work needed to be done.

Ever the optimist however, Whittaker could only see the positives. His number-one was someone he described as, "Arsenal's best ever goalkeeper."

George Swindin would himself become manager of the club in 1958 but as the war ended, he was in the middle of an eighteen-year playing career. He joined the club from Bradford City in 1936 and was firmly established between the sticks at the outbreak of the war. His post-war understudy was Ted Platt; Platt signed professional forms with the club in the few months before the war, but instead of fighting Swindin for the number-one jersey over the following years, he found himself fighting with the Royal Fusiliers in North Africa and Italy. He had to wait until November 1946 before making his full Arsenal debut against Leeds United, after Swindin picked up an injury.

Swindin was back in the side after half a dozen games and Whittaker had no hesitation in sticking with his number-one for the 1947–48 season. Any gloom and doom merchants were silenced when Arsenal stormed through the season, leading from start to finish and clinching their sixth League title. Key to this latest triumph was a signing made half-way through the previous campaign.

After a game at Everton in September 1946, Toffees' wing-half Joe Mercer came into the Arsenal dressing room to ask Whittaker to have a look at his injured knee. Mercer was England's wartime captain and had injured the knee in a match against Scotland at Hampden Park in April 1946. He had played on for the following months but the knee was becoming increasingly troublesome, and as his England trainer Tom Whittaker was in the opposing dressing room that day, Mercer thought it too good an opportunity to miss.

Whittaker inspected the knee and was shocked at how the muscles above and below the knee were wasted away; the knee itself was swollen and the

Arsenal manager told Mercer he was amazed that he could play in such a state. He told him to visit him at Highbury the next time he was in London. He was destined to be in London sooner than either of them thought.

Mercer was another player who had lost his prime years to the war. At thirty-two he was already considered a veteran; and a veteran with a dodgy knee is seen by many as a liability. So it was with Everton's manager Theo Kelly who dropped Mercer from the team in the autumn of '46. It wasn't long before Everton decided to place Mercer on the transfer list and the man from Ellesmere Port resigned himself to concentrating on his grocery business.

That was until Arsenal called and requested his services. Mercer described the transfer talk as the "shortest ever", so excited was he about joining the mighty Arsenal. Once it was agreed he could remain living in the North West – where he trained through the week with Liverpool, before journeying south – the deal was done. By September 1947 Mercer had assumed the Arsenal captaincy.

He took the job over from cricketer/footballer Leslie Compton. In a day and age where it was fairly common for players to participate in both the national winter and summer sports, he and his brother Denis played for Arsenal during the football season and Middlesex during the cricket season. Leslie would enjoy a twenty-two year Arsenal career and would become the oldest England debutant at thirty-eight.

The defensive line for the Gunners then consisted of international full-backs the versatile Walley Barnes (of Wales), Laurie Scott and later the classy Lionel Smith (both of England). At right-half was Scottish workhorse and vice-captain Alec Forbes. Forbes joined Arsenal from Sheffield United where he played against Carlisle in the third round of the 1946–47 FA Cup.

Not exactly impregnable, but as strong a defensive unit as there was throughout the top flight. And if you did get through them, then there were plenty of problems to face at the other end.

The playmaker in the team was the diminutive Scot and former brickie, Jimmy Logie. Logie was a similar build and background to Alex James who occupied the position during the '30s, and he would prove almost as effective during *his* career with the club. He joined Arsenal in 1939 only to see his career immediately stall with the outbreak of the war. He served in the Royal Navy before re-joining the club following his demobilisation.

The wing men were contrasting figures both in terms of profile and longevity with the club, but strangely, their playing records are not so dissimilar.

Freddie Cox (who won a Distinguished Flying Cross during the war) joined the club in 1949 after playing for North London rivals Spurs either side of the war. He enjoyed a successful, if relatively short, Arsenal career, playing less than a hundred games over the next four years.

In contrast, his wing twin for the first two of those seasons was a sporting icon of the day – Leslie's brother Denis Compton.

It is understandable that Denis will always predominantly be remembered as one of England's greatest cricketers, such were his exploits with the bat during the '30s, '40s and '50s. He was the original pin-up boy of British sport, following his signing of a lucrative sponsorship contract with Brylcreem (*in fairness, his 39,000 career runs also had a bit to do with it*). It is often overlooked however that he enjoyed an eighteen year career with Arsenal, first signing as an amateur when the great Chapman was still at the helm (he scored on his League debut against Derby in September 1936).

But like so many, Compton's football career was stop-start: struggling to establish himself in the outstanding team of the 1930s, then the war, plus injuries; it all meant that Denis would only make sixty starts for the club. Coincidentally, Compton and Cox both scored sixteen goals for the club during their respective careers.

As Compton's career on the wing was drawing to a close, Whittaker signed Don Roper from Southampton to replace him. Roper offered more than the role of provider, regularly taking up a central role that would see him contribute almost a hundred goals in his ten-year Arsenal career.

Not that goals from the flanks were desperately needed – the return from the Gunners' frontmen during the period was staggering.

Reg Lewis was the one constant. It's said by many that had it not been for the war, Lewis would probably have been Arsenal's greatest ever goal-scorer. As it was, he had to be happy with an official record of 118 goals in 176 games. (It should also be noted that Lewis scored a further 142 goals in just 128 wartime appearances.)

He scored 29 goals in 28 matches in the 1946–47 season and the Arsenal management team were keen to find someone as productive to complement him. To Whittaker's amazement, Jack Peart, the Fulham manager called him up and explained they needed money, so would he be interested in signing their craggy-faced veteran frontman Ronnie Rooke (he was 35). The Arsenal manager considered the offer for a good millisecond before driving over to Craven Cottage personally to seal the deal before Peart changed his mind.

 Rooke joined Lewis and the two led the way towards the Division One title the following year. Rooke spent only two and a half seasons at Highbury but returned an amazing 70 goals in 94 starts.

Whereas Rooke was a man for the here and now, Whittaker knew that he would need to keep an eye on the medium and long term. With this in mind, he signed two young forward players that few in the football world had even heard of.

Doug Lishman was twenty-four, six feet tall and an ex-marine commando. He was playing for Walsall when Whittaker saw him and saw him as a future focal point of his attacking line. If signing a player from the lower leagues raised a few eyebrows, signing one from non-League football had the football fraternity wondering if Whittaker was a genius, or if he had gone mad.

Butcher's assistant Peter Goring played up front for Cheltenham Town and was recommended to Whittaker by Jimmy Brain, who was a former teammate of Whittaker's from the 1920s, and who now managed the Gloucestershire club. Feeling secure with Lewis's experience and Lishman's power, Whittaker felt it was worth taking a gamble on Goring – another decision he never regretted.

In the dug-out meanwhile, Whittaker's right hand man was none other than '30s great Alex James, the midfield maestro so admired by fellow Scot Bill Shankly.

Inside the stadium in 1950

A friendly against Hapoel Tel Aviv in 1951 to test the brand new floodlights

Such was the club's renown, established through its pre-war success, foreign clubs queued up to play against the mighty Arsenal. Already established was an annual game against Racing Club de Paris, and their first post-war foreign tour came when they were invited to visit Portugal at the end of their latest Championship season.

The tour got off to an impressive start when the Gunners beat Portuguese Champions Benfica 5–0 in Lisbon. The second game however was a different story when complacency set in and the English Champions were beaten by a sub-standard Oporto side. After conceding an early goal, the Gunners were shocked to concede a further two in quick succession just before the break. Walley Barnes wrote of manager Tom Whittaker's fury at half-time and how he told his team they were endangering not only the club's reputation but that of the country as well!

A second half onslaught could only return two goals and the players skulked off to feel the wrath of their manager. At the post-match banquet skipper Joe Mercer congratulated the victors, whose manager could not hide his delight in talking up his team's performance:

> Everyone knows that Arsenal are English Champions and as English football is the best in the world, Arsenal must be regarded as *World* Champions. But now that Oporto have beaten Arsenal *we* have succeeded to the title of World Champions!

Such was local pride in the victory that a monument was hastily built and erected in the main square of the city to commemorate the victory! (It still stands there today.)

Embarrassing maybe, but the defeat failed to sully the club's high standing, and a year later these prototype Harlem Globetrotters received an invitation to tour the mythical football country of Brazil, who were preparing to host the World Cup finals the following year.

The invitation was made by Armando Barcellos, a millionaire building contractor who was instrumental in organising the tournament, and whose firm was responsible for building the amazing Maracana in Rio. He wrote to the Arsenal board suggesting that they travel to play a series of games in Rio and Sao Paolo against South America's finest as a warm up event to the international tournament that was to take place the following summer.

It took two days to fly to South America from London in 1949 (via Lisbon and Dakar). Upon their arrival, the visitors were greeted by hundreds of reporters and photographers who jostled with fans and officials. Barcellos hailed them as "*major maquina futebolistica do mundo!*" ("the greatest football machine in the world!").

The tour proved a great success and cemented Arsenal's stature in the world game. The one game they lost was against Vasco de Gama of Rio, the Brazilian champions. Whittaker later described them as "...the finest club side he had ever seen."

It was during this tour that centre-forward Peter Goring made his first team debut (scoring in the first minute against Flemengo). It was a prelude to an excellent season for the young man from Gloucestershire as the Gunners challenged on both fronts yet again throughout 1949/50.

Their efforts culminated in them reaching their fifth FA Cup Final where they faced Liverpool. (On the eve of the final, skipper Joe Mercer was crowned Footballer of the Year.)

As both clubs' colours clashed for the big game both were instructed to change – Arsenal chose gold shirts for the first time in their history. It proved appropriate as they dominated from the moment Jimmy Logie's defence splitting pass after seventeen minutes set up Reg Lewis who timed his run to perfection to slot the ball past Cyril Sidlow's left hand.

Arsenal 1950 FA Cup winners

Despite the heavy conditions the Gunners were slicking the ball around with ease and it came as no surprise just after the hour mark when Lewis struck again; Goring crossed the ball to Freddie Cox who flicked it on to the on-rushing centre-forward to crash in his second.

It proved a fitting end to the career of 32-year-old Denis Compton who collected his winners' medal, played the following week in the final League match of the season, and then retired from football. (The Comptons became the first brothers since 1876 to play in a winning Cup Final team.)

The Cup holders returned triumphant to Highbury and paraded the trophy round Islington before receiving a civic reception to commemorate their latest triumph.

They were the 'nation's club' with provincial newspapers reporting details of their annual finances (such a report was included in the *Evening News* of 22 November 1950).

Their next FA Cup tie was destined to be against Carlisle United.

Are We Nearly There Yet?

Although it was the first time that Carlisle United were to play at Highbury, two Carlisle teams had previously appeared at the famous stadium. A team representing the Carlisle National Union of Railwayman played two amateur cup ties against their London counterparts in 1920. Ominously, they lost both ties, but that was hardly going to put the current manager off.

It's not recorded what the weather was like in 1920 but the winter of 1950–51 was another unforgiving one, that left pitches around the country bone hard and it was through ice and snow that Shankly prepared his depleted squad for the big game. Even Highbury's magnificent facilities didn't stretch to undersoil heating in those days (it would be over fifteen years before that was introduced) and the game was in serious doubt up until seventy-two hours before kick-off.

Finally, on that Wednesday morning (3 January 1951), news came through from Highbury that the pitch down there was fit to play. The game was on.

On the same day the training at Brunton Park included a 5-a-side game that saw Fred Ford putting the players through their paces. Meanwhile Shankly himself supervised the fitness test of Geoff Twentyman (Twentyman had received a muscle injury against Accrington Stanley on Christmas Day and was a major doubt for the game). Twent came through the workout and barring any reaction between then and Saturday was declared fit to play.

The following day, Carlisle Secretary Bill Clarke travelled down to London to make final arrangements for the team's arrival. He met with Arsenal officials at Highbury to discuss his club's visit as well as the financial details associated with the tie. (If the crowd was to exceed the expected 50,000, the club would be in for a £6,500 pay day – a record by some distance.)

Shankly and his players train before the big game

Shankly puts Geoff Twentyman through his fitness test

Even frugal Carlisle United were therefore prepared to push the boat out for this once-in-a-lifetime adventure. And on this occasion, it would be the players themselves who were to benefit: not only were they to play at the best stadium in the country, under FA rules, the club could claim travelling and hotel expenses for players and officials alike. For a trip to London, United personnel were entitled to two full days' expenses (25s per day). Furthermore Bill Shankly informed his players that he would (within reason) cover any further expenses.

There would be 27 people in the Carlisle party comprising of 15 players (including a travelling reserve and three injured players who were treated to the journey), and club officials led by Chairman John Corrieri.

As players Phil Turner, Billy Hogan and Jack Billingham all lived in the Lancashire area, they were all due to travel from Manchester and meet their colleagues in London. Those colleagues meanwhile would travel on the midday train on the day before the game; upon arriving at Euston they would be taken to Mount Royal Hotel at Marble Arch where they were booked to stay on both Friday and Saturday nights.

The final treat for the players was a new kit. Upon his arrival at Carlisle, Bill Shankly famously burned all the kit that he described as "…an absolute disgrace!" For the biggest game in the club's history he had arranged for a new kit to be made for the players; and proudly emblazoned on the blue shirts was the city's crest.

On the eve of their trip south, Shankly took his players to the cinema to see *The Clouded Yellow* with Jean Simmons and Trevor Howard at the Lonsdale. Never one to miss an opportunity to fire up players and/or fans, during the interval he had arranged with the manager of the Lonsdale, George Forgham, to take the players on stage and introduce them to the 2,000-strong audience. Like the rest of the city Forgham had the football bug and acquiesced without hesitation.

Forgham and his wife may have been in on the act but no one else in the cinema was. One young man in the audience was keen supporter, 22-year-old Harry Notman. After recently ending his service in the navy Harry worked at the Co-op. He remembers today:

Bill Shankly supervises the packing the players' new kit for the trip to London

I was courting at the time. No one had any money so every Thursday, when it was half day closing, we used to make a bit of a day of it by going to the pictures. This particular night we had no idea what was happening. Usually at the interval, the usherettes would come out for people to buy an ice cream and then the organ would come up from the pit and everybody would have a sing-song. On this night all the lights came on and on to the stage walked Shankly – no one expected it. He introduced himself and said, "we're playing Arsenal on Saturday and these are the boys that are going to do it!" And he marched them on in turn.

Applause rang out for each player who the manager invited to the stage, but when the boss announced, "Ye' all know this local lad, and I can tell ye that Geoff Twentyman is fit tae play on Saturday." The Lonsdale erupted as though it was Brunton Park. Mr Forgham followed his guests on stage and wished them every success. Shankly responded by announcing:

> I can assure ye'all the team will take the field at Highbury suffering from no inferiority complex. They will play their usual clean, clever game and will do ye proud.

Mrs Forgham then presented each of the players with a white heather spray tied in the club's colours with a lucky horse shoe attached. (*Poor old Trevor Howard and Jean Simmons never stood a chance after the interval, so fired up were the audience.*)

The Historical Carlisle Pageant Publicity Committee meanwhile wanted to use the game to showcase the history of the county. They sought permission from Arsenal to allow local comedian Charlie Dixon to appear before the game in the guise of John Peel (grey and scarlet jacket, white riding breeches, black topper and hunting horn); he was to be accompanied by the Ireby Master of the West Cumberland Hound Pack. The plan was to lay a trail for the hounds and have them sprint the full length of pitch.

Charlie Dixon as 'John Peel'

Upon hearing the proposal, the hosts were more than happy to accommodate the unusual request and entered into the spirit by giving a resounding approval to their visitors.

While such arrangements were being made, the local newspapers were working on sketch maps of London, pointing out the main sights, giving advice of a tour route on the Saturday morning before the game for people who had never been to London before. The readers were even advised of the time of the changing of the guard in Whitehall. There were plenty of interested readers.

Despite the hard times, and the expense incurred by the recent Christmas holidays, the desire to travel to London was tremendous amongst thousands of fans. So much so that five special trains were ordered to take an estimated three thousand spectators down to Euston; a further train was put on standby that would go to St Pancras if required (the final figure would far outweigh the initial estimate).

Such was the camaraderie amongst work colleagues and their employers in the period, firms had commissioned coach and ticket packages for their employees. One fan who managed to book a place in a coach that was booked by the County Garage was Gerald Irwin. The 17-year-old had only been working for three months in the City Treasurers. A big Carlisle fan, Gerald sold programmes at Brunton Park and so attended every home game – first team and reserves. He explains the circumstances of his travelling arrangements:

> It wasn't terribly expensive either because the trains in those days were considerably cheaper than what they are now. And I think all the firms in town booked a coach on the train to give their employees the opportunity of going. I went on part of the train that was booked by County Garage, where my brother worked. He didn't go to the match – at the time there were two players working at County Garage Norman Coupe and Geoff Twentyman, so he worked with both of those and he was a panel beater as they were. I suppose they did other things at County Garage but I never met anyone who did

anything other than panel beating! I've a feeling the tickets were all part of the package – tickets and train fare.

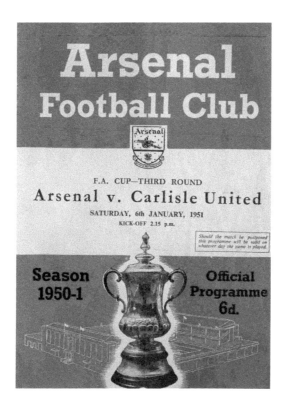

Another fan was Ronnie Jones who travelled with his neighbour Sid Scott:

> I remember it cost £2 to travel down to London. We set off at midnight – the trains were slower than they are now so it was probably about eight o'clock by the time we arrived.

One fan to miss out was Harry Notman, who had little money and had to work Saturdays. But for every hard luck story, there seemed to a heartwarming tale of people helping the less fortunate. Fred Nugent of Scalegate Road spent most of his young life suffering intense pain, due to a spinal complaint. Fred was a big Carlisle fan but was unable to afford the price of the journey and ticket. That was until he happened to be attending a whist drive when the organiser asked if he was going. Upon hearing his negative reply, she organised a whip round amongst the whist players and raised enough money for Fred and his friend Jock Sneddon to go on the trip of a lifetime.

As cup fever gripped Carlisle and the fans were sensing a great adventure, some of the players were playing down their chances. Jim MacLaren's landlady told him that she and her husband intended to travel down to London to see the big game. "I wouldn't bother," replied the phlegmatic MacLaren, "you don't want to waste your money going down there just to see us lose!"

Paul Daley meanwhile was successful in convincing his dad Claude to take him to London. Rather than try and get places on the Euston trains however, Claude made alternative arrangements with his employer. One of the Leyland DAF vans belonging to W.B. Anderson was in need of repair and as such, the plan was for Claude, his son and a driver to take the van down to Leyland in Lancashire on the day before the game. Once it was repaired, the three would then drive on to London through the night and attend the game on the Saturday.

Claude Daley with wife Nora and youngest son Rodger in the early 1950s

Despite the small number of cars in these pre-motorway days, hundreds of others were planning to make the same 300-mile journey.

One of Paul's former primary school teachers at St Bede's school, Anne Donnelly, was also intent on travelling. Anne came from a football family with her father playing for Carlisle United before moving down to Swindon in the 1920s. Her brother Bob lived in London following his war service and also intended to see his home-town team play in the capital.

(Anne duly travelled to Highbury with some friends for the game and, without arranging to see her brother – or even knowing he was attending – bumped into him outside the ground among the tens of thousands of people!)

Claude Daley and his son Paul meanwhile made the three-hour road journey to Leyland in the dodgy van, twenty-four hours before kick off. Upon their arrival, imagine the young lad's horror when his dad learned that the van could not be repaired, as it was in need of a part that the garage didn't have. It may get them back to Carlisle but it could not make the six hundred mile round-trip to London. They weren't going to make it!

After much fretting they set off back to Carlisle, Paul believing that his dream was over. Unknown to him at the time, because all the special trains had been over-subscribed, it was decided to run the spare train to St Pancras – if the driver could get the van back to Carlisle, there was still a chance they could make it.

Back *in* Carlisle, free travel warrants were issued to 700 railwaymen but one man who missed out was Train Crew Supervisor and avid fan Sam Kirk. Sam was on nights the first week in January 1951 and knew he would be unable to make the journey himself. Instead, once on duty at around eleven o'clock, it was his job to supervise the departure of the special trains:

> I saw them all off, there were hundreds of them! I even saw my sister-in-law Ivy who was going down to the match with her husband. I remember everybody was really excited.

People of all ages were gripped by the adventure. Three brothers, Jim, Bob and Eddy Nicholson had travelled down to the previous round at Southport; they took their mother, 70-year-old Anne, offering her the opportunity to go shopping along the classy Lord Street. Instead, Anne requested she go to the game with her boys and became completely hooked – come the Arsenal tie, nothing was going to keep her from Highbury!

Every coach of every train was crammed full to capacity, with stories of children (and small adults!) occupying the overhead shelving as every conceivable space was taken up.

Claude Daley and his son Paul *did* make it back to Carlisle in time and Claude secured them a place on the St Pancras train. They were going after all!

Paul Daley (eighth from the left in glasses and cap) with some school mates at the station in the early 1950s

As far as the club was concerned, it was to be the first time Carlisle United had travelled to London since 1910 when they played West Ham in the Cup (which was the third consecutive year that Carlisle had travelled to the capital in the first round of the FA Cup: 1908, Brentford; 1909, Fulham).

As far as many of their fans were concerned, it was to be their first ever trip to London. Their uncomfortable six or seven hours' travelling was to be offset by the excited atmosphere on board.

At around six o'clock the following morning, the specials carrying the weary travellers started rattling into Euston. Gerald Irwin's memories of that morning are mixed:

> We went across to the East End of London to an aunt of mine where a pal of mine and I got some breakfast. Then we set off for the ground and I've no idea of what we did – haven't a clue; we must have done something because we would have left my aunt's house at 11:00 or 12:00 and travelled to Highbury.

At 10:00 the Nicholson brothers took their mother Anne to see the changing of the guard at Whitehall. Regardless of the game she was about to see, Anne seemed bowled over by the spectacle:

> I had never been to London before. I didn't think I would ever have cause to go now! But to see the soldiers and the horses – and all that colour, I couldn't believe what I was seeing! It was wonderful.

Ronnie Jones made his way to the ground with his friend and neighbour Sid Scott. Upon their arrival they found a local entrepreneurial photographer who was offering to take pictures of the Carlisle supporters as they enjoyed their big day. Ronnie recalls:

> He took our picture and told us to meet him at the same place after the game. He must have had a studio close by where he could develop the pictures while the game was on because when we came out, sure enough, he was there with a queue of Carlisle fans all buying their souvenir picture.

The special train carrying the surplus of fans to St Pancras duly arrived, much to the relief of Paul Daley who was going to see the match with his dad Claude after all. At the ground Paul stared in astonishment at the wonderful art-deco stadium that was *literally* three hundred miles from Brunton Park, but *figuratively* a million miles away from the facilities for spectators and players alike. This was the stage on which the biggest game in Carlisle's history was to take place. And around eight thousand lucky citizens were there to witness it.

Ronnie Jones (right) and Sid Scott in London on the day of the game

The Game

The 1950–51 season started well for Arsenal. With only two defeats in their first nineteen league games, the Gunners found themselves in their customary position at the top of the First Division as the Christmas period beckoned.

Amid the *team's* success came individual International recognition for three of their defenders in the same match. At the incredible age of thirty-eight, centre-half Leslie Compton made his England debut in a 4–2 victory over Wales on 15 November 1950. Alongside him at left-back was fellow debutant and team mate Lionel Smith, while for the opposition was Welsh centre-half Ray Daniel. (Daniel signed for Arsenal after the war and made his first team debut in May 1949. A year later and he was pressing Compton for his regular place in the side; coincidence then that they should both be selected to make their International debuts against one another. Team mate Walley Barnes also played for Wales in the same game.)

To cap a wonderful autumn, Armando Barcellos again invited Arsenal to tour Brazil at the end of the season (an invitation to play in Russia would soon follow). So around the time that the Arsenal players were dreaming of playing in the Maracana in Rio, the Carlisle United players were slogging through the mud of less glamorous locations like Gresty Road and Sincil Bank.

Such grounds, along with Holker Street and the Park Avenue Ground, were the usual destinations for those United fans who could afford to see their team play on the road. So it is difficult to fully comprehend the excitement they would have felt at the thought of seeing their team play at a stadium rivalled only by Wembley for its fame and grandeur.

As well as the expected eight thousand travelling Carlisle fans it was estimated that they would be bolstered by several thousand Tottenham Hotspur fans whose team was due to play away at Huddersfield on the same day (it was commonplace for Arsenal and Tottenham fans to travel to each others' ground to cheer on the opposition when their own team was away from home! Again, this is confirmation that there was little else to do.). Scores of ex-Cumbrians who lived in and around the capital were also known to be attending.

One of the latter number was a Mr W.E. Reay who regularly visited Highbury to watch Arsenal play. He wrote an incredibly prophetic letter to the *Carlisle Journal* during the week prior to the game entitled 'How to win at Highbury':

> United should not leave their Third Division tactics behind them. Arsenal's win at any price policy means lots of hefty charging, sometimes not always according to the rule book. My theory of how to crack the Arsenal defence is to use the wing-forwards as much as possible. The defensive system adopted by Arsenal appears to be designed to stop penetrating inside-forwards, and if the outside men hold the ball until reaching the bye line before centring, the defence, as in the Burnley game, is caught on the wrong foot.

The game Mr Wreay was referring to was a game three weeks' earlier when Burnley had travelled to Highbury and gone away with a 1–0 victory. (It was the start of a period where Arsenal would stutter in their quest for League honours.)

Further credence was given to the theory when it is considered that on the day of Carlisle's cup triumph at Southport (9 December), Arsenal played out an epic 4–4 draw with Blackpool, in a game that saw the great outside-right, Stanley Matthews run riot. It was a performance that prompted Tom Whittaker, the Arsenal manager and long-time admirer of Matthews to try and sign the winger (unsuccessfully as it turned out) and it was a game in which defender Walley Barnes remembered in his autobiography:

With those bewildering runs and two-way body swerves of his, he flummoxed three or four of us at a time, opening the way for two equalizing goals.

As the holiday League programme drew to a close, morale was suddenly low amongst the London giants; their dip in form had seen them slip to third in the League. In *his* autobiography, Whittaker described his depression at the period:

> One of the blackest Christmases I can remember at Highbury meant no goals and no points, to bring our record to only one point (the Blackpool game) in six games, and it finished with Douglas Lishman breaking his leg in an almost unbelievable accident. In avoiding a tackle he sat down heavily on his ankle as if squatting on the ground.

Doug Lishman was one of Arsenal's first choice front men, having displaced the previous season's cup final hero Reg Lewis. Lishman sustained his broken leg in the 0–3 League defeat against Stoke on Christmas Day. So by a strange quirk of fate, both sides suffered key striker injuries prior to the big game – Jackie Lindsay breaking his jaw against Barrow, and Lishman breaking his leg against Stoke.

Significantly, Arsenal suffered another key injury in the Stoke game, this time at the other end of the field. First choice goalkeeper George Swindin was hurt in a collision that was destined to rule him out for several weeks.

The Carlisle party arrived safely in London on Friday 5 January and enjoyed a comfortable night's sleep at the Mount Royal Hotel. After breakfast, on the day of the game, and after taking an opportunity to stretch their legs around Marble Arch, they climbed aboard their coach that was to take them across central London to Highbury.

Already there to meet them were hundreds of Carlisle fans; their blue and white favours the only splash of colour among the dark clothing that matched the dull grey day. Making their way through the fans and into the empty stadium, Shankly had arranged for a tour for his players before it opened to the fans. Billy Hogan later recalled that the boss was already start-ing with his motivational psychology:

> The boss got us all wound up before the game, walking us round the pitch in a then empty stadium, reminding us of some of the great players who played there. He would say, 'These English defenders Smith and Mercer, both lucky men to be playing football. I would never sign them, they aren't good enough for Carlisle United. You boys are here because I want you here. Let's get rid of this lot and get into the next round with no fuss.'

It was all designed to wind up his players, of course. Literally speaking, it was nonsense – both Shankly and Mercer held each other in the highest regard. When Shankly was appointed manager of Carlisle, Mercer wrote generously (and prophetically) to his long-time opponent and friend:

> I must write you a few lines of congratulations and good wishes on your recent appointment. I hope most sincerely that your career as a manager will be even more successful than that as player. In my humble opinion, no player ever gave as much to his club, country and football as you.

Kind words from a giant of the game who was destined to become a good manager himself. Shankly held Mercer in equally high esteem later saying "Joe is a gentleman, full of humour and steeped in the game. Joe is a real man."

But on *this* day, nothing less than the full character assassination would do!

The stadium Shankly was showing his players around boasted flood-lighting apparatus and a state of the art broadcasting control room – in con-junction with the BBC – in order to broadcast any game played there. (This would be greatly appreciated by those back home in Carlisle who couldn't afford to make the journey. They would witness the club's first ever 'filmed' game in the local cinemas.)

Loud speakers were a fixture throughout the ground for the purpose of controlling the spectator traffic. From his box, where the whole stadium could be viewed, the chief steward was in a position to instruct all of his staff at the turnstiles when to open, and to announce to the crowd outside where admittance could be best obtained.

That crowd, and the atmosphere, was now building. While the players had been safely tucked up at their hotel, the convoy of trains had rolled into Euston between six and seven o'clock that morning.

Now, two hours before kick-off, thousands of Carlisle fans were milling about the stadium and when the turnstiles opened, the blue and white hoards streamed through. Claude Daley took his wide-eyed son through the marble-halled underbelly and then out into the open air where he had secured tickets for the lower tier of the East Stand.

Carlisle fans inside Highbury

It is estimated that they were two of eight thousand Carlisle fans, and with the addition of several thousand Tottenham fans cheering for Arsenal's opposition (*regardless of who they were*) it all promised to be a cracking day. So much so, that it wasn't just the ordinary folk from Carlisle whose imagination had been captured by the glamour tie – the great and the good were there too.

One of the bi-annual meetings of Commonwealth premiers happened to be taking place in London in January 1951. By way of a break in high-level political discussion, the Australian and New Zealand Prime Ministers (Robert Menzies and Sidney Holland respectively) attended the game between the greatest club side in the world and the tiny minnows from the north of England whom no one had really heard of. They were joined in the Directors' Box by the Lord Mayor of London.

The match programme provided the dignitaries with a useful overview of the obscure opposition. It pointed out that the Blues remained unbeaten on their own ground all season and had only dropped two points from twelve matches. And out of their fourteen away games they had lost only four. 'This produces an excellent record of having scored nearly 80 per cent of the highest number of points possible,' the editor concluded.

As the politicians and celebrities were being wined and dined in the executive suite, prior to taking their seats, and the tens of thousands of fans were streaming through the turnstiles below them, the players were taking in the luxury of the dressing rooms.

The spacious, tiled facilities had an adjoining bath room, with hot and cold plunges, spray and needle baths and the latest apparatus for treatment of injuries.

With underfloor heating throughout and a special treatment room for trainer Fred Ford to attend to knocks, most of the players had never (and would never again) experienced such luxury.

There were however two exceptions among the Carlisle number (apart from Shankly himself of course, who had guested for Arsenal during the war). Paddy Waters had played at Highbury for Preston almost two years earlier in March 1949. North End had achieved a creditable goalless draw in an otherwise dismal season that saw them relegated from the top flight.

The other player to experience the Arsenal Stadium was stand-in striker Jack Billingham. Billingham had lined up for Burnley in a crunch match at Highbury in February 1948. The game was significant as Arsenal and Burnley were lying first and second in the League as the season went into its final third. 62,000 flat caps and dark overcoats filled the stadium that day (it was estimated that there were 20,000 locked out) and witnessed a 3–0 home victory which meant that Arsenal ended the day eight points clear of their Lancashire rivals. They went on to win their first post-war title by seven points, whilst Jack and his team mates finished the season in third place. Now, Billingham was here again, not in the claret of Burnley but the blue of Carlisle United.

It is now half an hour to kick off and over 58,000 are in the stadium. George 'Twinkletoes' Baxter wanders round the cinder track waving OLGA as the away fans cheer him on.

Twinkletoes and Olga entertain the fans before the game

Out on the pitch, the Metropolitan Police Central Band are entertaining the crowd with a varied programme including works by Schubert, Delibes and Ivor Novello. They end their programme – much to the delight of the travelling fans – with a rousing rendition of '*John Peel*'.

It's a moment that strikes a sentimental chord with John Ross, a Carlisle lad who now lives in Walthamstow and who later writes:

> I cannot express the feeling I got of homesickness when I saw the Blue and White colours splashed among the vast crowd. Supporters could be seen in all parts of the ground. I must confess a lump came to my throat when the band struck up '*John Peel*'.

Under the iconic white clock at the south end of the ground, stands Charlie Dixon, resplendent in scarlet jacket, black topper, while dog handlers manoeuvre the West Cumberland Hound Pack along the goal line. Once the ground staff has laid the trail down the full length of the pitch, the signal is given for 'John Peel' to give a blast on his hunting horn: the handlers release the dogs who race down the pitch towards the North Bank terracing at the opposite end of the ground.

The crowd explode into an excited roar at the sight. The Arsenal fans could be forgiven for thinking this will be the amusing highlight of this regulation Cup tie against these hicks from the sticks.

The hounds about to be released

In the Arsenal dressing room, there is a calmness that precedes most games such is their confidence and experience. Manager Tom Whittaker has made a couple of enforced changes, with the injuries to first choice keeper George Swindon and centre-forward Doug Lishman. In their place comes reserve stopper Ted Platt and Cup Final hero Reg Lewis (not bad replacements: Platt is already an experienced 'keeper, while Lewis has over a hundred goals for the club). Interestingly Whittaker makes another change at centre-half, preferring Ray Daniel to the more experienced Leslie Compton who has a slight injury. It will be Daniel's first FA Cup tie.

Down the corridor in the away dressing room, the anticipation and excitement is almost unbearable. Shankly is unrelenting in his motivational rhetoric.He gets wind of Whittaker's selection and latches on to the inclusion of Platt and Daniel. "*Reserves! There just a bunch of reserves!*" he cries at his players.

He has spent the last week convincing his team the impossible is eminently probable. Now he emphasises the point only this time his phrases were punctuated with expletives – the casual routine obscenities of the dressing room.

His game plan is to use the speed of inside-forwards Jimmy Jackson and Phil Turner to upset the Arsenal defence, allowing wing men Alex McCue and Billy Hogan to create havoc down the flanks. It's Billy Hogan especially who the manager is banking on to give the underdogs a chance. Hogan later recalled the feeling in the dressing room:

> The boss kept at it right until kick-off. We were all a bit in awe by then as you could now hear the crowd inside the stadium. As we got up to walk out of the dressing room, Shanks grabbed hold of me and said 'Billy, that Lionel Smith is nothing, understand? Nothing! Get at him and get round him every time, you will terrify him with your skill, show him up for what he is, okay?"

Shankly then repeats the instruction to Hogan's team mates to get the ball to Billy at every opportunity. It is five past two and the bell sounds for the players to leave the dressing room. Shankly's oration has such an effect on his players it could have been delivered in another context by Churchill or Shakespeare's Henry V (Paddy Waters: "We felt ten feet tall after listening to Shanks"). He takes one last look at his charges before they walk out and delivers his final skin-prickling words of inspiration:

> Whatever happens on the field today lads, you are going to go out of this dressing room a credit to the City of Carlisle.

Alex McIntosh heads the line of players: right out of the dressing room and along the corridor before turning left into the tunnel. Then it's out onto the field and into a wall of noise generated by almost 60,000 spectators. (Billy Hogan: "I was amazed to hear shouts of Carlisle everywhere – it was wonderful stuff.")

The Blues break off towards the Clock End, leaving the home side to take to the field and warm up in front of their favoured North Bank stand. Joe Mercer duly leads his men out and the volume is turned up even further.

After a few minutes of both teams jogging and drilling to get warm on the cold, damp afternoon, the shrill of referee Bill Rogers's whistle summons Mercer and McIntosh to the centre circle for the toss. Both skippers meet and shake hands cordially. Gentleman Mercer tosses the coin and gives his opposite number the honour of calling: the underdogs have their first victory of the day. Remembering his manager's instruction, McIntosh chooses ends and opts to attack the Clock End in the first half, thus depriving Arsenal of attacking their favoured North Bank in the second. (Classic Shankly: anything to upset the opposition.)

The teams change ends and at 2:15pm on 6 January 1951, Mr Rogers gives another blast of his whistle and the game that the whole of Carlisle had been eagerly anticipating for a month is underway. The explosion of noise sends shivers down the spine of many a Carlisle fan (young and old) who have never experienced such an atmosphere before.

Arsenal have the ball and spend the early seconds holding it and passing it between defence and midfield. A minute passes before the first Carlisle player touches the ball – Paddy Waters intercepts a through ball by Jimmy Logie and clears to touch. Cue cheering from home fans who anticipate an attack, and away fans who are relieved that the first parry of the mighty Arsenal is thwarted.

Joe Mercer and Alex McIntosh at the toss up

It is three minutes before Carlisle get some meaningful possession and incredibly it leads to the first effort on goal. Jimmy Jackson plays a neat pass outside to Alex McCue who crosses first time, and it is the ever-willing, stand-in centre-forward Jack Billingham who beats Daniel in the air. With Platt struggling, it is the other Arsenal full-back Walley Barnes to the rescue as he heads clear at the near post.

Walley Barnes clears Jack Billingham's early header

The effort acts as a wake-up call for the home side who start to stream forward. First it's Roper who leaves McIntosh on his backside and crosses for Goring and Lewis, but the assured Twentyman is there to clear the danger.

Another Arsenal effort sees Jimmy Logie produce a flicked back header that almost puts Reg Lewis in, but Jim MacLaren dives and smothers at the centre-forward's feet. Then, with MacLaren out of his goal, Freddie Cox slides a pass through for Logie; the little Scot can't get to it and Norman Coupe is on the Carlisle line to shovel the ball away. The passage of play is closely followed by a scramble in the visitor's box that sees McIntosh slice the ball and he and MacLaren look on helplessly as the ball skews away and misses the near post for a corner.

Norman Coupe scrambles the ball off the Carlisle line

(McIntosh later recalled, "I turned to Geoff Twentyman and said 'we're going to lose 20–0 at this rate.'")

The corner is cleared and for the first time, Carlisle succeed in following their manager's key instruction to get the ball out wide to Billy Hogan. Immediately, Hogan controls the ball and gives his beleaguered defenders some respite. He turns and carries the ball forward and with a drop of the shoulder, rounds the advancing Lionel Smith and forces an interception from the captain Joe Mercer, who has to concede a corner.

It is the first of three corners in quick succession for the visitors. *"UNITED! UNITED!"* The travelling fans cry as their team are slowly growing into the game after the early onslaught.

Back come Arsenal as they settle into their delightful passing game for which they were renowned. Logie, Cox and Roper are all prominent in the first quarter of the game. But then increasingly, so is Hogan. His poise is rubbing off on his team mates and confidence is growing all the time in the Third Division outfit.

Twenty minutes in and the novelty is wearing off for the Arsenal fans – despite their team playing decent football, they are now being matched by this team that they've never heard of. And that right-winger is now making England left-back Lionel Smith look a little bit silly. Hogan continually weaves this way and that rendering Smith powerless.

After several minutes of seeing his colleague struggle against the tricky winger, skipper Joe Mercer moves across to give greater assistance. Incredibly this only serves to inspire Hogan further; his ball control is impeccable, and his twists and turns are delighting the crowd. By pulling Mercer slightly out of position, it is opening up space for Phil Turner to operate inside. Hogan is now waltzing past Smith and Mercer and linking with Turner who is causing concern in the Arsenal box.

Man of the match Billy Hogan takes on Lionel Smith in the first half

Ted Platt saves a Phil Turner effort as Barnes looks on

Another Hogan run and feed to Turner sees the inside-right produce a lovely feather touch to Billingham who fires in a shot from outside the box that just clears the Arsenal bar.

Then Carlisle's momentum is broken when Paddy Waters sustains a leg injury; in severe pain, he is helped to his feet by Geoff Twentyman and Fred Ford but has to hobble off, hanging on to the trainer. Shankly directs his troops from the side-line and instructs inside-forward Jimmy Jackson to drop back and take Waters's position at left-half while the Irishman receives treatment in front of the dug-out.

Jackson slots in and immediately intercepts a pass by the dangerous Logie. The ten men appear to be driven on by the blaring hunting horns that sound around the great stadium; instead of dropping back while numerically disadvantaged, they continue to utilise the skill of Hogan. In the thirty-fifth minute, it is Hogan's wing twin Alex McCue who fires in a cross shot that has Platt scrambling across his goal line to concede a corner.

Before it could be taken, the Cumbrians are buoyed at the sight of Waters who hobbles back on to the field. Jackson resumes his position at inside-left. The corner is whipped in and cleared by Arsenal vice-captain Alex Forbes but before his teammate Peter Goring can control it on half way, Tommy

Kinloch leaps into the tackle to win possession back; he goes left to Waters who finds McCue again on the left. The winger sends in another high cross shot and Platt causes consternation among the home fans by fumbling the ball; fortunately for the goalie, Jackson is on the wrong side of him to take advantage and the relieved Welshman manages to smother the ball.

Paddy Waters tussles with Jimmy Logie

For the first time in several minutes, Arsenal now build through midfield with Forbes and Logie; the final ball through to Goring is cut out again by the magnificent Twentyman whose positional sense is of the highest order, but the ball breaks to Reg Lewis who fires in a stinging shot that Jim MacLaren pushes over the bar.

It was cut and thrust for the remainder of the half with both sides playing scintillating football. Carlisle United were matching the mighty Arsenal in every department and as the whistle blew the whole stadium rose to applaud Shankly's men off the field.

The boss can't wait to get into his players: hyper with excitement and expectation he firmly believes his team are going to win the game. Inevitably, he turns to Hogan:

Billy *san*, you're killing that full-back. He disnae know if he's coming or going. (And then to the rest of the players) Gae it tae Billy at every opportunity.

In the annex of the trainer's room, Paddy Waters is in agony as he lay on the bed and Fred Ford manipulates the injured calf muscle.

The Arsenal fans must be believing that the minnows from the North have shot their bolt and the blue-bloods will take control, having had their first-half scare.

Not a bit of it – upon the resumption, United pick up where they left off. With the first action of the second half, McIntosh plays a deliberate pass down the right wing to that man Hogan. Billy holds it and then spins, beating Smith in the process; Mercer comes across but the winger then steps inside and takes him out of the game. Right-back Walley Barnes is drawn across to shepherd Hogan wide while Smith and Mercer recover, but Hogan still manages to find a pass through the three Arsenal defenders to Turner whose speed takes him past the centre-half Daniel and force a smothered save from Platt.

Hogan is proving a nightmare for the Arsenal defence: when he receives the ball deep with his back to goal, he spins, jinks and invariably beats Smith in one movement; the England man is having a torrid time trying to keep him in check. When Billy receives the ball whilst moving forward, on the other hand, his swaying running and interchange between feet has Smith and Mercer mesmerised.

It is at this point that Arsenal appear to change their formation as they look to seize the initiative for the first time in the match. The two wing-halves, Mercer and Alex Forbes are noticeably pushing up when in possession creating a seven-man attack; the tactic drives the Carlisle midfield back and isolates Hogan (hopefully, Smith, Daniel and Barnes between them can contain the wizard).

The tactic works for more than ten minutes as they batter away at the Carlisle defence with brute force in the case of Goring and Forbes, and scheming dexterity in the case of Logie and Cox.

Reg Lewis beats Jim MacLaren in the second half but his header goes wide

Either way, the Blues defence remains intact: McIntosh and Coupe are disciplined and hold their shape, while Kinloch, Twentyman and Waters look like giants as the game progresses. The two front men Goring and Lewis are struggling to make any impact.

And when Arsenal do get through, Jim MacLaren is playing with great authority: a tip over from Roper; a diving interception from Cox; and point-blank stop from Alex Forbes from a rare corner are among the highlights.

The calm assuredness with which Carlisle are playing belies their position two divisions below their hosts. An example of their confidence is evidenced on the hour mark when Paddy Waters has to leave the field for the second time to receive more treatment on his injury. Jimmy Jackson again slots back in as if he were born to the position.

If there are any nerves being shown as the game moves into the last quarter it is by the Arsenal defence who simply can't handle Hogan. With Carlisle having weathered the quarter-hour storm, they seek to get their offensive work back on track.

Platt punches clear from McCue and Jackson in the Arsenal goalmouth

As they kick towards the North Bank, Hogan is operating [on the right] in front of the two benches; Shankly is in his ear the whole time shouting encouragement to his star man, whilst making sure that the beleaguered Smith hears a few derogatory comments in the process. Every time Carlisle win possession in midfield, the manager can be heard at pitch level above the din of the crowd, "*Gae it tae Billy, gea it tae Billy!*"

Increasingly, the normally stylish defenders who specialise in moving the ball through midfield to set up the next attack are happy to shovel the ball back to Platt and out of harm's way.

There are destined to be two seminal moments in the tie: if either goes Carlisle's way, it will see the Cumbrians pull off the biggest cup upset in the history of the competition.

The first comes deep into the second half; another slick passing move involves Twentyman, Jackson and Billingham; the Arsenal defence is split apart and Jimmy Jackson lifts a bouncing ball through to Phil Turner who finds himself clean through in the box with defenders watching on helplessly. Although the moment is over in a flash to some in the ground, to others, time seems to decelerate into a strange slow-motion sequence.

Turner is onto the ball in a flash and fires in a volley from no more than eight yards out (later described by one report as a 'pile-driver'); as it flies towards the top right hand corner, Ted Platt the Arsenal goalkeeper, whose momentum has been taking him to his left, somehow manages to hurl himself backwards and twist in the air in order to sweep the ball over the crossbar.

The millisecond of silence as nearly sixty thousand people held their breath is followed by a comingled explosion of relieved and anguished noise.

Ted Platt pulls off a wonder-save to stop Phil Turner winning it for Carlisle

It would be the closest Carlisle would come to scoring on this amazing day. From the corner, Jimmy Jackson rises above his marker but heads wide.

With the game entering its final ten minutes, Arsenal's fitness and strength appear to finally be telling.

The diminutive Jimmy Jackson has almost run himself to a standstill; the lion-hearted Paddy Waters has played for almost an hour with an agonising muscle injury; now Tommy Kinloch picks up a similar injury. The Carlisle forwards are all starting to drop deeper to help their defensive colleagues.

Arsenal can now sense an undeserved victory, as they push forward looking for the late winner.

Carlisle fans are now watching their heroes fearing a cruel sting in the tail. Young Paul Daley sits in the lower tier of the East Stand with his dad (he recalls today, "I couldn't take my eyes off the big clock above our goal – I'm sure it was going backwards!).

He wasn't alone: Jim MacLaren is performing heroics in the Carlisle goal as the home side press for a late winner. (He later said the same thing to his daughter Maggie, "They had this big clock behind the goal. Every time the ball went out or we cleared it, I turned round to check how long was left!")

The famous Highbury clock behind MacLaren's goal

Arsenal scramble, and indeed gamble for position. Carlisle clear but tired minds carelessly surrender possession and back they come. But Arsenal's play is now speculative as they go in pursuit of knock-downs and ricochets, trying to manufacture a victory from the dogged minnows.

Freddie Cox steals half a yard on McIntosh and sends in a cross, while Twentyman, Kinloch, Lewis and Goring jostle for position around the penalty spot. The ball comes over and the imperious MacLaren comes off his line and punches clear – the third such effective clearance during this commanding performance.

MacLaren aided by Kinloch and Twentyman leaps above Reg Lewis

The ball comes in again and Norman Coupe shovels it behind for an agonising last-minute corner. Don Roper runs across to take it while his colleagues twist and pivot in the box as they seek to slip their markers. But the Carlisle defence stands firm; as the ball is cleared for a throw in Mr Roger's whistle sounds through the dull afternoon air and the Blues have achieved their greatest ever result.

Bill Shankly marches on to the field with his arms raised (in what would become a familiar pose) to greet the eleven heroes. Behind him, Paddy Waters collapses in agony and has to be carried off the field by Fred Ford and Geoff Twentyman; a hero amongst heroes.

The players have executed the manager's game plan perfectly; moreover they have produced a prototype Shankly performance that was destined to be the hallmark of his future great sides. They had run hard and fast; they had tackled for their lives; they had continually forced the game, without trying to reinvent it; they kept it simple when they had the ball; they worked tirelessly when they didn't.

For Arsenal it was a goalless draw and a chance to fight another day; for United it was a moral victory. They had held the cup holders by sheer skill and courage. The whole stadium rose to applaud their incredible effort.

Shankly was immediately approached by a reporter and asked for his initial thoughts. His response was characteristically self-assured:

> It is a wonderful result and it came as no surprise to me. I knew the lads would pull it off, and they themselves felt the same way. The result is all the more praiseworthy because we were playing against one of the most formidable teams in the game.

The post-match analysis by the players was unanimous in the acknowledgement of Carlisle's effort and the work of Billy Hogan in particular. Geoff Twentyman later said:

> No one could take it away from Billy Hogan that day. He was able to get the ball and keep possession, which gave all of the other players time to move into space. He had the beating of defenders so the other forwards had room to work.

As for the man himself, he modestly reflected years later, while recalling the mind-games employed by the opposition he had humbled:

> I did just as I was asked and felt I did all right. Afterwards, both Lionel Smith and Joe Mercer came up to me and said I was the best forward they had come across that season, but nobody would get two chances to make fools of them. I didn't really understand what they meant by it then and I laughed it off.

This was an incredible admission from the Arsenal defenders who had been run ragged by Stanley Matthews only a month earlier. Mercer would later go on to have a successful career in management (most notably with Manchester City). When asked some years later, he remembered the Carlisle tie vividly:

> It was always going to be a tricky tie. As I remember, Billy Hogan was the star of the game: he gave poor Lionel Smith a real roasting, it was as though he was floating on air at times and the ball seemed so comfortable attached to him! I can not recall any other player doing that to Lionel. Carlisle were unfortunate as we were ill-prepared for the actual football style, which was way above what we had expected. They could have caught us out had our 'keeper not been on top of his game.

The following week, Arsenal were at home again to Middlesbrough. As the programme for the game was printed before the Carlisle replay took place, it could not comment on the final outcome of the tie. However, the editor was equally generous as Mercer in his praise of the visitors:

> Whatever the result was on Thursday, Carlisle played good football last Saturday and there is no doubt that they deserved every bit of their right to play again. There was no question of Arsenal being unlucky. We had our chances and did not take full advantage of them and if anyone was unlucky on that day, undoubtedly it was Carlisle.

(Carlisle United were destined to make two further visits to Highbury, this time in the 1970s. On both occasions they gave a good account of themselves but never quite matched the class of '51 – they narrowly lost both games.)

THE HEROES RETURN

An hour after the final whistle, many fans were still milling around the stadium, trying to take in what they had just witnessed while eeking out every last bit of the experience. Besides, they knew they had to wait several more hours before they could get their train for the long return journey north.

(As with the arrangements twenty four hours earlier, all the special trains were delayed until around midnight to allow the normal railway traffic to go about its business as scheduled.)

Like Ronnie Jones, some fans queued to receive their photograph taken before the game. Ronnie's future brother-in-law Bill Scott meanwhile turned his attention to other matters. He had received his call up papers and had received permission to join up later that night. Bill therefore travelled from Carlisle with the rest of the hordes, watched the game and promptly went off to do his national service.

Others decided to make a night of it. Gerald Irwin – the young lad from the City Treasurer's Office, who worked weekends as a programme seller – and his friend went to see a show:

> In the evening after the game the trains didn't leave until midnight, so my pal and I went to see *Babes in the Wood* at the London Palladium. I can't remember why we chose that particular show but we had to do something to fill the time. I think it cost about 1/6.

The players meanwhile didn't have to worry about any overnight trains. Regardless of the result it had been agreed that they would spend a second night in London and travel home in relative comfort the following day.

The feeling in the dressing room was one of euphoria as it began to sink in exactly what they had achieved. The first rapturous response they received upon leaving was when they stepped out of the front doors of the wonderful stadium to climb aboard their coach, waiting to take them back to Marble Arch. Still outside were hundreds of Carlisle fans who fired up their horns and rattles once more at the sight of their heroes.

Back at the hotel, some players decided to spend a quiet night while others chose to follow the lead of some of the supporters. One of the heroes of the afternoon, goalkeeper Jim MacLaren arranged to meet his brother and together they went to see *The King and I* in the West End. Shankly had told his players that he would – within reason – cover any expenses they incurred during their stay in the capital. The frugal MacLaren therefore thought he would enjoy a night out at the theatre at the expense of the club and his manager.

Gerald Irwin and his friend left the Palladium after *their* show and made the short journey across London to Euston. The first trains pulled out at eleven thirty.

It's difficult to imagine how many of the fans must have felt that night. The vast majority of non-service personnel had never been to London before. Now they had made their excited journey to the capital, seen the sights, been part of an almost sixty thousand-strong crowd – with all the noise and the involuntary rocking and swaying that that entails – and witnessed the greatest performance by any Carlisle United team.

Ecstatic? Proud? Perhaps even a bit overwhelmed at the last twenty-four hours? Probably all of those things but above all else, I'm guessing just plain tired!

Three hundred miles north, reports of what had happened were at first sketchy. At the time of the kick off (2:15pm) a crowd had gathered by the *Evening News*' office in English Street, where regular updates from the game were to be telephoned through. The crowd grew as the game went on and almost inevitably rumour and counter-rumour about how it was going started to ripple through the two-to-three thousand strong gathering. At one point, a report had it that Phil Turner's goal-bound volley (that produced a wonder-save from Ted Platt) had actually gone in! (Half of English Street were probably having a street party by the time the report had been rectified!).

Finally, it was confirmed to the whole city on the radio that the game had finished goalless and United had secured the greatest result in the club's history. Even more exciting for those who missed out on the trip to London was the thought that they now had an opportunity to see the mighty Arsenal in the flesh, as a replay was now required at Brunton Park.

As several thousand fans tried to get some sleep on the train, and tens of thousands back home went to bed dreaming about the return fixture, the presses in Fleet Street were running in preparation for their Sunday readership. They turned out to be fulsome in their praise of the Blues:

> The toast should be Carlisle – magnificent Carlisle! Often they were brilliant and had the Arsenal defence running around chasing shadows. Carlisle were indeed a revelation. *News of the World*

> Carlisle sprang one of the biggest sensations of the FA Cup by holding Arsenal to a draw at Highbury, and they thoroughly deserved their replay. *Sunday Sun*

> If they (Carlisle) had won, it would have been no more than the comparative quality of their football deserved. Hogan was the best of the ten forwards on the field. He dribbled like Matthews but more directly. *Sunday Times*

> Carlisle United proved to the mighty Arsenal the old soccer maxim that 'the Cup is a great leveller.' Their draw at Highbury was the feat of the day and a feather in the cap of manager Bill Shankly. *Sunday Pictorial*

Fifty per cent of the artistry in this thrilling match was shown by the visitors, so much so that it was impossible to tell, except from the colours of the shirts, which was the side with the big reputation.
Sunday Express

By the time the early morning editions were hitting the newsstands around the country, the special trains were rattling into Citadel Station carrying the fans who had witnessed the historic event. Their eye witness accounts, along with the press coverage prompted the city to visit the station later that day to witness the arrival of the players. People started to gather by mid-afternoon.

In London meanwhile, the players were oblivious to the activity back home. They breakfasted and boarded their train that pulled out of Euston at around ten o'clock. One player in particular wasn't necessarily thinking about the welcome that awaited him and his colleagues. Instead Jim MacLaren was more interested in his manager repaying him for his theatre tickets the night before. (His son Stuart recites the tale that MacLaren mithered Shankly all the way home but never got reimbursed yet – much to his dad's irritation!)

Two hours prior to their arrival in Carlisle, fans had started to congregate on the north-bound platform in anticipation of a glimpse of their returning heroes. Initially a few score, the numbers gradually increased to a couple of hundred. Once the platform was filled (*I'm not sure what any travelling passengers were supposed to do!*), supporters started backing up onto the bridge that overlooks the main north and south-bound platforms.

The bridge became full which forced any newcomers to onto the platform opposite leading to the main entrance. When the whole of the interior of the station was full, onlookers started to congregate outside in Court Square; then – despite the cold, damp day – back towards the Crescent and between the twin rotundas and into English Street. At first some well-intentioned spectators did their best to keep off the grass and avoid the flower beds in front of the Courts, but through sheer weight of numbers, and the realisation that the raised area was too good a vantage point to pass up, the ornamental gardens were soon trampled into a muddy bog.

News came through that a landslide in the South of England had delayed all northbound rail traffic and the players' train would therefore be over an hour late. No one seemed to mind – by this point there were over twenty thousand people in and around the station waiting to greet them. The crowd outside now included many who had been to the game the previous day. They had been home to snatch a few hours of sleep and were now back in position, still proudly sporting their blue and white favours and carrying their horns and rattles.

The railway police had sent out a request for assistance to the *city police* force and thirty officers joined their railway colleagues in trying to control the crowd and keep a pathway clear for traffic. There was never any fear of trouble at this point, but the volume of people threatened to overwhelm the city centre.

Harry Notman had been at the Lonsdale Cinema the previous Thursday night to hear Shankly give his rallying cry. He was also there in the early evening darkness to witness the incredible scene of the players' return:

> It was an incredible sight. There were crowds of people all around Court Square, up English Street and down Botchergate. It was like VE Day!

As their approaching train was announced – almost two hours late by this time – the murmured anticipation on the platform started to ripple throughout the station, into the square outside and beyond. When it came into sight, the murmurs turned into cheers; and when it halted on the platform and the players appeared at the windows of the train, cheers turned to roars as the sound wave travelled outside and exploded with the sound of horns, bugles and rattles.

The fans greet the arrival of the players...

...who stare bewildered through the windows

They then try to disembark!

Mayor Partridge greets Bill Shankly and his players

The players were flabbergasted by the reception. For the first time in eight hours, Jim MacLaren's attention was taken from mithering his manager about shelling out for the theatre tickets the previous night. The goalkeeper later told his daughter Maggie, "When we arrived it was amazing – you'd have thought we had won the cup!"

Among thousands on the platform was the Mayor, Cllr Albert Partridge, resplendent in ceremonial chain, along with the Town Clerk of Carlisle Corporation. Bill Shankly was the first to step down followed by his players and the rest of the party. The Mayor shook the manager by the hand and took his prepared statement out of his pocket. Trying to make himself heard above the din, he announced:

> On behalf of the citizens of Carlisle I give you a most hearty welcome back to the Border City and at the same time extend to you all heartiest congratulations upon your wonderful achievement at Highbury. It was no mean task to hold the mighty Arsenal to a draw on their own ground and in so doing you have fulfilled the dreams of thousands of your ardent supporters. I am very sorry indeed that I myself could not be present at the game, but have read with pride the glowing tributes that the national press have seen fit to pay to the skill, spirit, determination and grit that you displayed before some 58,000 spectators.

> Carlisle is no mean city. It is justly renowned throughout the world for many reasons, but today the county will recognise her as a city that can produce a football team of which any town, city or county could be proud.

Then singling out the manager himself continued:

> And now a word to your manager Mr Shankly. I am sure there is no prouder man in Carlisle at the moment and that everyone will

recognise the important part that he has played in bringing about this happy and well-deserved result.

I am told that the hospitality at Highbury left nothing to be desired and if I may, I would add my word of appreciation of everything done on your behalf. We in turn shall give them a rousing welcome on Thursday.

I am confident that the football will be good and I trust that the boys from Arsenal, their manager, directors and supporters will, whatever the result of the match, retain happy recollections of their visit to Carlisle.

One young lad who had sneaked into the station early and secured a prime view on the bridge overlooking the platform was 12-year-old Jazza Boyle:

It was the biggest thing the city had ever seen – it was fantastic. I have a picture at home of me looking through the trellis bridge over the platform. To see the players trying to get off the train and through all the people was incredible.

There have been royal visits to the station over the past hundred-plus years; there have been the arrivals of US Presidents; and there have been men going off *to*, and coming back *from* wars. But no event had ever (or subsequently *did* ever) rival that of the return of Shankly's men that late Sunday afternoon in January 1951.

Once the initial ceremonies were over, the problem of getting the players through the seething masses had to be overcome. A coach had been positioned at the entrance to the station to take the players back to Brunton Park but it was another half an hour before the party managed to pick their way through the jostling crowd one-by-one, amid handshakes and backslaps.

The players pick their way towards the exit

The bemused Hounds pose outside the station

Once on the coach – in spite of the damp, darkening afternoon, and much to the delight of the spectators – the coach had a detachable roof that was pushed back, allowing the players to stand on the seats and wave to the adoring public as they crawled through the crowd. What was intended to be the final leg of their trip back to the ground had turned into a full-blown city centre victory parade, amid the din of horns and bugles.

Upon their arrival back at Brunton Park, no time was wasted in preparing for the replay which was four days away. The two wing-halves Paddy Waters and Tommy Kinloch had received serious leg muscle injuries, and they were immediately sent for specialist treatment.

Treatment continued on the two players (and on Geoff Twentyman and Alex McIntosh, who had also received knocks) the following morning. A local reporter ('*The Rover*') went down to Brunton Park to interview the manager about his team's prospects. Granted, his team had just pulled off an amazing result but they were still about to face the biggest club in Europe. Shankly self-belief however was unswerving:

> Our prospects for the replay are excellent and I would say we are now favourites to win on Thursday, if our injured can recover in time.

> (*Favourites!*)

In light of the recent injuries that threatened to deplete his injury-hit squad still further, Shankly assessed his options and looked at the players who might have a chance of playing on Thursday, should he be forced to change his team.

In one throw of the dice, he actually dispatched Jackie Lindsay to an electro and manipulative therapist in Sheffield. Dr Cornelius Swain examined Lindsay's jaw and, following treatment, suggested he had a chance of playing.

Along with the rest of the country, the doctor appears to have been caught up in this national football story when he wrote to Jackie. In his letter he appears to be more interested in the game than on Lindsay's injury.

The letter sent from Dr Swain to Jackie Lindsay

Dear Jack

Just a line to wish you all the best against the Arsenal.
Just get stuck into them, you can do it. Tell your teammates this. I
shall be waiting to see the results and I hope you win. So again, all the
best Jack and good wishes to all.

Yours sincerely
Neal

(Alas, the doctor's optimism was misplaced: Lindsay never responded to the treatment and it would be a further two weeks before he would be fit to play again.)

In the Monday evening edition of the local paper, *The Rover* covered the game that had taken place forty-eight hours earlier, Shankly's assessment of his team's chances in the replay, and a characteristically generous tribute from Arsenal skipper Joe Mercer of his opposition:

> Three times our scouts had seen Carlisle since the draw was announced and their verdict was that they were a good side, endeavouring to play football all the time. So we were well prepared, and we went out on to that field determined to go all out for victory. Carlisle nevertheless shocked us by the excellence of their football and held us. It was a great performance.

Little did the United fans know as they were reading this that this would be Mercer's last involvement in the tie. That day he came down with flu and was ruled out of the replay – manager Tom Whittaker would need to re-shape his defence to cope with Hogan and Turner.

If the tie wasn't the talk of the town already, it certainly was now – and things were just about to be cranked up a notch.

The players and manager weren't the only important cargo being transported north following the big game. Arrangements had been made with *Pathé* News beforehand to film the game and the Lonsdale Cinema had secured rights to show the film in the week following. When the proposal had first been mooted, most thought it would be of novelty value. But now, after the stunning result and the forthcoming replay mild curiosity had developed into frenzied excitement.

Crowds, crowds, crowds!

Crowds had travelled down to Arsenal in the first place, crowds had flocked to the station to see the players return, and now crowds were queuing outside the Lonsdale to see highlights of the game. (The biggest crowd of all was still to come.)

On his and his players' unscheduled visit to the same theatre, Shankly had promised the audience that his boys would give their all. In the same theatre a matter of days later, the audience were about to see for themselves just how much they had given.

The audience sat mesmerised at the flickering black and white images of the *Pathé* News film – some more than others.

One, heavily pregnant, young woman had travelled down to the game with her husband, father, brother and his wife. Her mother had expressed concern that she shouldn't be going in her condition. The daughter re-assured the mother by telling her that while the lads were going to the match, she and her sister-in-law were to spend the day shopping in London. Imagine the mother's reaction then when she went to the Lonsdale with *her* sister, only to see her pregnant daughter on the big screen in the front row at Highbury cheering on the team as though her life depended on it!

The narrator's precise, clipped BBC accent of the period simultaneously filled Carliseans with pride and humour:

- *"An early scare for the visitors. Looks like you're in for a long afternoon Mr Shankly!"*
- *"The underdogs – or should that be hounds – start to find their feet. Perhaps John Peel has inspired them after all!"*
- *"Another fine save from goalkeeper MacLaren – clearly he's had his porridge this morning!"*
- *"It's that man Hogan again – he's got the Arsenal defenders spinning like tops!"*

Eric Thompson was an apprentice engineer with Pratchett Brothers in Denton Holme and was one of the hundreds who saw the game on the big screen. Eric had gone to the Creighton ("a rugby school" as he recalls) but had caught the football bug late in his school years. He remembers it vividly today:

We saw the highlights of the game in the Lonsdale. Watching Billy Hogan waltzing past two or three of their defenders was wonderful. We were just about gasping at the sight. Unbelievable!

The anticipation grew as the hours and days passed. Every angle was now being covered and everyone was taking advantage of the feel good factor – one shop window on English Street displayed a sign that screamed at the passers-by: *'Two astounding draws! Carlisle United v Arsenal and ROUTLEDGE'S SALE!'*

On behalf of the city, *The Rover* was virtually camped out outside Brunton Park as the week wore on, waiting for news of injuries and possible team selection, as well as waiting for the next words of wisdom from the great man.

As with the preparation for the game in London, no break in routine took place. No training took place on the Monday following their return (they obviously played well enough to be excused!), but on Tuesday and Wednesday the squad were back to it, training as normal.

On the Tuesday morning, the news of Waters and Kinloch was promising – both were responding well to treatment and stood a good chance of playing. If either didn't make it, Spud Hayton would probably deputise as other possible replacements Dennis Stokoe or perhaps Alec Scott were still recovering from injury.

When Shankly wasn't available, the reporter was badgering chairman John Corrieri and secretary Bill Clark for comments. As well as enjoying their fifteen minutes of fame, the Carlisle officials knew that the whole tie would deliver the biggest windfall for the club since the Ivor Broadis sale.

On the day before the game, Waters and Kinloch were out on the training field to be put through a rigorous fitness test by Fred Ford and supervised by Shankly himself.

In truth, Waters and Kinloch (as well as Twentyman and McIntosh) would require treatment right up to the kick off the following day, but following the workout, they were declared fit to play. Shankly named the same team that took to the field at Highbury on Saturday and used his final statement to fire up the fans still further:

I think with Waters and Kinloch fit we have a very good chance to win. The Arsenal will have more respect for us now than before the last match because they now know the ability of the team and what they can really do. I am looking forward to another great game and as I said before the last match I am sure the team will do justice to themselves. I know the supporters will be with us and the 'Brunton Roar' is as good as a goal start.

Between training, treatment and interviews, Shankly and his players had to deal with hundreds of letters and telegrams from all over the country, congratulating them on their performance at Highbury and wishing them well for the replay. Oh yes, and the other thing: *asking if they had any tickets!* The players had only been allocated a few tickets each and relatives and close friends had already taken up that allocation, but that didn't stop people trying it on.

The players were not just inundated with requests by post; they were stopped in the street and bothered at home by people with just one question on their lips…

Got Any Spare Tickets?

If the effort of the Carlisle players in holding Arsenal to a draw has become acknowledged as being remarkable in subsequent years, then the scramble for tickets for the replay among fans has become legendary.

On the Monday morning following the players' return, a meeting took place between the Chief Constable of the city police force William Henry Lakeman, Bill Clark the club secretary and Corporation officials to decide an acceptable ground-capacity for the game, and the logistics of selling the tickets. Their decisions would result in confusion, humour, anger and near-tragedy in equal measure.

The replay was to take place on Thursday afternoon (half day closing) with a kick-off time of 2pm (no floodlights in those days!). It was agreed to build temporary scaffolding at the back of the Warwick Road end of the ground that would increase the capacity for the game to 22,000. Significantly, and understandably, the match would be an all-ticket affair.

Although hosting Arsenal would be the biggest event in Brunton Park's history, the game itself would not be the first of its kind. Two years earlier Leeds United had visited Carlisle at the same stage of the FA Cup; the match attracted almost 23,000 spectators, so presumably the city officials convened believing that this wasn't anything they hadn't seen before.

The big difference here of course is that the Leeds game had been a home draw with plenty of advance notice. This Arsenal game on the other hand was an unforeseen replay that had to be arranged at short notice (no one really expected Carlisle to get a draw in the first match).

Clark informed his colleagues that Arsenal had confirmed that they would be taking their full allocation of 2,000 tickets, and representatives from several other Football League clubs had made applications to attend, such was the level of interest within football of the second instalment of this David and Goliath clash.

It was therefore agreed that the remaining tickets were to go on sale to the public on a first-come-first-serve basis the following day. With Tuesday being a normal working day, and in anticipation of (mainly male) supporters working all day, it was further decided that the sale would commence at 7pm; and instead of selling the tickets at Brunton Park, they would be distributed from the Covered Market in the centre of the city.

This meant that Charlie Hetherington, the Market Superintendent, would make the necessary arrangements, amongst which was the recruiting of various personnel to help with the distribution. As Charlie used to work in the Treasury Department of the Corporation before taking up his current role, whenever there was a need for extra staff he would invariably go back to his old department to ask for volunteers.

One willing volunteer was Gerald Irwin, the 17-year-old junior who sold programmes on match days and who had been one of the travelling thousands the previous Saturday. He had only worked in the Treasury Department for three months but jumped at the chance of being involved in the continued adventure.

Chief Constable Lakeman agreed to make twenty police constables available to keep an eye on the queue, just in case it stretched the length of Fisher Street and round on to Corporation Road. So, everything was in place – what could possibly go wrong?

The arrangements were announced to the city in the *Evening News* that night:

> There will be various selling points and the correct amount of money must be rendered in order to facilitate quicker distribution, which will be undertaken by Corporation Staff. Queues for tickets will be formed outside in the Market Street entrance to the Market and the exit from the Market will be by the Scotch Street entrance. The prices

of admission are 5s for the stand, 3s for the enclosure and 1s 6d for the ground.

Much to the annoyance of season ticket holders, they were given no guarantee of a ticket for the game – they would have to queue like everyone else. Evidence of the authorities' gross underestimation of what was to follow came in the form of their final statement:

> Should the full supply of tickets not be disposed of on Tuesday night, the sale of tickets will be continued on Wednesday night.

Despite the homecoming scenes at the station on Sunday evening, it seems as though the city officials still didn't grasp the magnitude of attention the event was generating. The novelty of a few weeks ago when the draw was made had manifested itself as a ripple of excitement in these austere times; a novelty that might allow the lucky few to escape the humdrum. Now – after Shankly had fired the city up and his boys had achieved the near impossible seventy-two hours earlier - the ripple of excitement had developed into a frenzied tsunami of interest. Everybody wanted a piece of the Carlisle/Arsenal magic.

The morning of Tuesday 9 January was cold and damp, in keeping with the time of year. The first people appeared on the corner of Market Street and Fisher Street at 6am, a full thirteen hours before the doors of the Market Hall were due to open.

As the hours ticked by, the queue steadily grew: a handful turned into a couple of dozen; *it* turned into a few score; and *it* turned several hundred by mid-morning that stretched down the length of Fisher Street.

Claude Daley gave his son Paul some money for a ticket the night before – the plan was for the young lad to go to school and then make his way to the Market afterwards. Claude meanwhile would go to work at W.B. Anderson's as normal; then home for some tea, and off to the Buffs on Fisher Street for his usual Tuesday night at the club.

One of Paul's classmates was Brian McGough and he had a less subtle plan – he was to play truant and make sure he was towards the front of the queue when the doors opened. (Brian would duly get a ticket, only to be told when he got home that he had to give it up for his older brother Tommy. Seniority ruled in those days I'm afraid – Brian never got to see the game!)

It became apparent by late morning that the majority of the queue was made up of women. The authorities had assumed that men would be at work and then come down to the Market afterwards; the men certainly *were* at work but they had arranged for their wives and mothers to get a place in the queue before relieving them and taking their own place, at the end of the working day. Many of the women brought their knitting to while the hours away, whereas others brought stoves to keep themselves warm. And as the day went on, the inevitable musical hall songs were given an airing. (Those were the days – if in doubt, have a sing-song!)

The start of the queue at Fisher Street

One young man who made such an arrangement with his mother was Eric Thompson, the apprentice engineer at Pratchett Brothers in Denton Holme.

And when you didn't have a non-working relative to save you a place, you relied on your seniority, as young Kenny Woods found out. Kenny was a telegram boy at the Post Office and on Tuesday 9 January he went into work to receive some good news and some bad news. The good news was that he was to be excused his normal duties of cycling around the city delivering telegrams; the bad news was that he was to get in that queue outside the Market Hall until his supervisor finished work, at which point he would be sent home.

Gordon Lawson meanwhile was another schoolboy at the Creighton School:

> It was the only time I played hooky from school. Me and my friend Maurice (Moggy) Johnson were supposed to be back in school at 1:30pm and we nicked out. We joined the queue right outside the Working Men's Club at 1.35pm.

Gerald Irwin on the other hand, was one of the volunteers who would be distributing the tickets later that night. At lunchtime he walked back to his house in Denton Holme to get some sandwiches together for his evening shift. On his way back to work he decided to look at the queue to see how it was shaping up:

> When I saw it I remember thinking, 'That's a recipe for disaster' because of the way it was shaped. The queue went from Fisher Street to Corporation Road. The queue had a U-bend in it because there wasn't enough room for people to stand.

By 4pm on the mid-winter's afternoon, the light was fading and a six-deep queue of dark-clothed people snaked their way for over two miles from the Market Hall like a Lowry painting.

And on it goes...

Paul Daley finished school as scheduled and made his way, full of excitement, to the Market. Once there, he found himself walking away from the Market along Fisher Street, into Corporation Road, across to Dacre Road and round the Castle embankment. "I joined the queue at the signal box on Devonshire Walk," recalls Paul today.

And he wasn't the last to join: as afternoon morphed into early evening and the working day ended, more people joined, taking the queue up Devonshire Walk past the slaughter-house and on to the Caldew Bridge. It was by now, pitch dark.

Finally, when the doors of the Market Hall opened at 7pm, it was estimated that there were over 25,000 people in a three-mile queue, waiting to get in.

Behind the giant doors of the market, Gerald Irwin and his colleagues sat at trestle tables with mountains of tickets. Charlie Hetherington was supervising his charges while Chief Constable Lakeman and his deputy Blacklock stood behind keeping an eye on proceedings.

Outside, the customary cheer went up, as always accompanies the end to such a long wait. A surge of people in their excitement created an initial rush, causing the sale to stop almost before it had started. Lakeman called his small group of constables to the front to restore a little order which allowed the sale to re-commence.

Water-tight security inside the Market Hall!

For almost an hour the long line of ticket hunters wandered in to claim their prize. Then at approximately eight o'clock, all hell broke loose as dozens of queue jumpers joined the queue on Fisher Street from Long Lane causing people to be lifted off their feet and carried through the giant doors. Three distribution tables were knocked over as tickets, money and people littered the floor.

There were minor injuries with people being trampled and others fainting after waiting so long in the first place, and then taken by the shock of the surge from behind. One of the latter victims was a young secretary from Cavagan and Gray's food factory. Like many an office junior she had been instructed to take her place in the queue and get two tickets.

When the poor girl fainted she was carried into a safe area to be tended to by some concerned officials. After a few minutes of said officers leaning over her, she showed signs of regaining consciousness. "Can we get you anything, young lady," asked one of the officials. She looked up through bleary eyes, obviously recalling the stern instruction received from her boss at 'Cavvies': "Two tickets please!" she mumbled.

What started off as an orderly queue gradually developed into chaotic disorder that rumbled along the length of the people-train. Paul Daley had inched through the inky blackness for over an hour and had just about made it round to the junction of Fisher Street and Finkle Street when he heard someone shout "They're closing the doors!" This caused mayhem all along the street as people scrambled to get what they thought were the last few tickets.

Inside the Market Hall there was confusion as to what was going on outside. Gerald Irwin again:

> My dad was a copper and was in civvies in the queue and when the queue broke he went home and put his uniform on because he thought there was going to be a riot. We were all told to pack everything up as we were going to be sent home. So we handed everything in and left.

There was certainly a need for extra police resource; reports followed that it was responsible members of the public who attempted to form a cordon to prevent a full scale crush taking place, while others escorted women and youngsters away from the danger.

With the doors closed, gradually the panic subsided and the thousands of people who remained in what was left of the queue began to dissipate, either through disappointment at missing out, and/or relief at being unhurt. One of that number was Paul Daley who walked home broken-hearted at not getting a ticket after standing for so long.

As the night wore on, and with the hubbub outside apparently subdued, the officials in the Market re-opened the doors; the reason the hubbub had subsided is that the vast majority of people had gone home – there was virtually no one *outside!*

As word spread that the doors had been re-opened, people started to drift back and buy their tickets in relative comfort. One such person was Claude Daley who rolled out of the Buffs on the opposite side of Fisher Street and only a few yards from the Market. He walked into the giant hall and casually bought a couple of tickets to take home for him and his son, who believed his chance had gone. ("I couldn't believe it when my dad told me what had happened," he recalls today.)

At a quarter past eleven the sedate sale was stopped with three hundred tickets still unsold.

One that had been sold was purchased by a young woman who worked as a junior clerk/typist in the Co-op Funeral Directors. Like many women she wasn't a big football fan, but like everyone else she got caught up in the excitement that gripped the whole city and decided to queue for a ticket with a few friends. Having stood most of the day she duly picked up her ticket in the first hour of the sale.

At work the following day, all of the talk amongst her colleagues was about the tickets, the replay; the whole event. Her supervisor was a football fan and wanted to go to the match but, unlike his young assistant, hadn't queued for, or purchased a ticket. All of the football-chatter in the office made him hanker for a piece of the action all-the-more. He therefore offered the young woman twice the face value of her ticket; after considering the offer, and given that she was not a big football fan, she decided to accept it: he got a ticket; she made a bit of extra cash.

Now, being a good Catholic girl, the young woman was at mass later that day and happened to be relating the sequence of events to her friend Ellen Donnelly afterwards. She was overheard by an old-school fire-and-brimstone Curate, who interrupted the conversation and made his displeasure known at the 'transaction'. "What you did was tantamount to stealing!" he told the poor woman, and instructed her to give half of the money back to her supervisor the following day.

It was a day and age of yes-father-no-father-three-bags-full-father, and the young woman (presumably after a restless night) went into work the following morning with the intention of reimbursing her colleague. When he heard her story he found it highly amusing and refused her money, telling her that she deserved it after queuing all day. It therefore ended up with the football fan getting his ticket, the young woman having her Catholic guilt assuaged, and the Curate not knowing any different. (I suppose the moral of that particular story is that when it comes to football, the Lord really *does* move in mysterious ways.)

The remaining tickets went on sale on the Wednesday morning at ten o'clock – by quarter past they were all gone and the game was officially a sell-out.

That same morning one of Eric Thompson's colleagues at Pratchett's (let's just call him George to spare his blushes) found himself in the boss' office explaining his absence from work the previous day. "I wasn't feeling well boss, I had to stay at home all day," explained George in all earnest.

The *following* morning George found himself back in the boss' office explaining how his picture appeared in last night's newspaper with him proudly posing for the camera with his ticket for the big match after queuing all day!

It was only one of the dozens of recriminations that went on following the fiasco. The local papers were inundated with complaints about the lack of organisation, the policing, the allocation system, the venue, and just about anything else that came to mind. And when the authorities weren't being blamed for their collective ineptitude, the press themselves were being pilloried for fuelling rumour and counter-rumour.

The event was christened 'Black Tuesday' by one newspaper, while letters to the Editor poured in. One from Bernard Hunter from Harraby graphically describes the terror:

'Barbaric Scenes in the ticket queue.'

Sir – the near trampling and chaotic behaviour of persons at the sale of Cup tie tickets has been subject of letters from myself to Mr Hargreaves MP and the Chief Constable of the City Police Force.

I stressed the near suffocation and near trampling of elderly and young people in the 8:30 rush along Fisher Street. It was a barbaric scene with police constables apparently helpless to assist or alleviate the matter.

The crowd of about 6,000 surged against the market door, holding and wedging innocent persons in their wake, whilst constables (I saw no sign of senior ranks) stood and surveyed the scene from the perimeter of the 6,000-strong swaying mass.

The crowd of 6,000 people had no control over their individual movements but were propelled to the Market entrance and squashed for about an hour until they were propelled through the market door.

Their main desire for the previous hour was no doubt one of let's go home, I'm feeling ill. But with an excruciating pressure from all sides and no police help outside the Market (despite around 20 PCs watching) one had no option but to await the pleasure of the surging crowd and be literally slung through the Market doors – gasping and half dead.

It seems the whole event had succeeded in upsetting everyone, especially season ticket holders, one of whom wrote:

> It wouldn't be so maddening if half of the queue were regular Carlisle United supporters but many of them have never in their lives watched a football match. I think season ticket holders should have first chance of the tickets for this big event.

To casual supporters from outside the city, one of whom from Penrith suggested:

> Sir – it is regrettable that much of the credit brought to Carlisle by the splendid display of their football team has been destroyed by the disorderly scenes and official ineptitude of Tuesday night.
>
> That a good number of people who profess to appreciate sportsmanship and disciplined endeavour at Brunton Park do not carry these attributes into their daily lives is a great disappointment.

The Chief Constable tried to make a statement by way of explanation, in which he used phrases like, 'unprecedented crowds' and 'unanticipated disorderly conduct.' But that didn't really wash with the populace who remained unconvinced and disappointed in the authorities' seeming inability to organise an evening's merrymaking in a licenced premises.

An inquiry was demanded of the Watch Committee, to look into the disgraceful scenes, but when it was announced that any inquiry would commence the following week – by which time the replay would be over and done with – enthusiasm for heads-to-roll started to wane and attention started to turn again towards the match itself.

And it wasn't just the fans who were thinking about the game. The beleaguered Chief Constable of Carlisle, William Lakeman was meeting with George Routledge and George Bowman, chairman and secretary respectively of the Publicity Committee of the Carlisle Historical Pageant on the night before the match. The two Georges were angling for a repeat of the scarlet-coated huntsmen and the hounds that had taken place on Saturday and had proved so popular with Carlisle and Arsenal fans alike.

Lakeman was suggesting that the crowd didn't need any further incentive to be wound up: the arrival of the players on Sunday, the ticket shambles on Tuesday, and then the arrival of the Arsenal party (which was taking place as they were meeting). The hounds trailing over Brunton Park might cause more problems than it was worth. The organisers pointed out that it was *Pathé News* who had requested the spectacle for inclusion of their newsreel scenes. The meeting ended with a nervous Lakeman agreeing to 'John Peel' leading the hounds onto the field before the players but for no trail to be laid across the pitch.

As the final three hundred tickets were being sold in Carlisle on that Wednesday morning, three hundred miles south, 2,000 tickets were being sold for the same match at a far more leisurely pace. Carlisle-born Frank Ribchester was standing outside Arsenal Stadium at 6am. He could have treated himself to a lie in: by the time the ticket office opened at 10am there were only about fifty people behind him in the queue. A steady stream of supporters moseyed along Avenell Road to purchase as many as they wanted. By noon, the full allocation had been sold.

In the *Evening News* that same night, a lone voice cried out for some attention:

'Less Soccer!'

Sir – Monday's *Evening News* contained nothing but nonsense about Carlisle United. There was no news worthy of the name in it. This football madness is really alarming to the ordinary citizen and one wonders why you as the Editor would allow it. A sense of proportion is the vital possession. Surely one column would do the Carlisle team ample justice.

Furthermore this waiting for tickets all day is worthy of a better cause surely. Pleasure! Pleasure! What has come over our people? Would they show the same keenness to help one another in any small way? I wonder.

I am a regular reader of your paper but I must say I am more than disgusted at this pandering to sport. Work has to take second place to it when our country is struggling for its very life. I write this in no malicious spirit but as a strong protest against this arrant nonsense.

Please give us more news and less football.

But nobody listened. The whole city was high on a cocktail of cup fever, and with all the tickets sold (by fair means or foul) everything was in place for the biggest sporting event the city had ever seen.

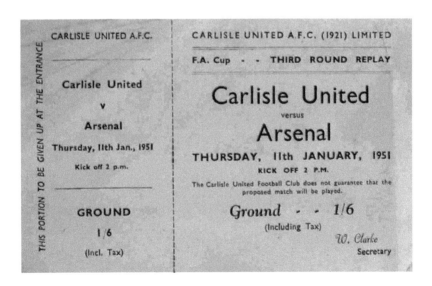

Pure gold dust

THE REPLAY

On Wednesday 10 January another crowd – this time two thousand plus – filled Court Square outside the station. Their curiosity was pricked by the arrival of the opposition: the legendary Arsenal were due to arrive shortly after seven o'clock.

The Mayor and Mayoress were again present, as was the Carlisle United Chairman John Corrieri and Bill Shankly, to greet their auspicious guests.

Station officials – fearing a repeat of the ticket fiasco the previous day – refused to allow anyone into the booking hall and platform after six o'clock. That didn't stop dozens of opportunists sneaking in beforehand however to hide in toilets and to wander across to the more remote parts of the station.

By the time Tom Whittaker stepped down from the train to introduce his men to the welcoming party, the platform resembled the scene that had taken place seventy-two hours earlier when the United party had returned from London.

As the visitors assembled on the platform to shake hands with their hosts, a voice was heard to cry from the back of the platform, "Up the Arsenal!" No doubt that's exactly what Shankly was thinking (*"Aye, right up the Arsenal!"*).

Their coach was moved round to the Victoria Viaduct entrance in a an effort to avoid the crowd outside the station; word soon got out however and two thousand curious on-lockers scurried round from the main entrance to see them leave for their short journey to the Crown and Mitre Hotel. Hundreds lined English Street and traffic was stopped to allow the

Arsenal party through. In the foyer of the hotel, Whittaker was met be a local reporter and asked for a comment about tomorrow's game:

> We are looking on this match as of equal importance to any match we have ever played, because Carlisle United put up a great show at Highbury, and they are worthy opponents of any side in the country. I fully expect Carlisle to win the Northern Section Championship this season.

The party then dined at the hotel and turned in around ten o'clock. An hour or so later three hundred miles south, a train carrying seven hundred Arsenal fans prepared to make the long overnight trip north.

As the newsreels of the original game had proved successful with the local audience, it had been decided to follow suit with the replay. But whereas Highbury's state of the art facilities accommodated such modern-day technology, the modest Brunton Park did not. Temporary gantries were therefore hastily erected above the Paddock on the west side of the ground to capture the action of the second game.

On the morning of the match the Arsenal team breakfasted at around nine-thirty and followed it with a gentle stroll around the city centre. Whittaker and his staff meanwhile set off for Brunton Park to have a look at the ground and, particularly, the pitch. Like the previous Saturday, it was overcast and in all probability, the pitch would be heavy. This point was put to Whittaker the previous evening but he expressed his comfort at the prospect, believing his team "…would be quite at home on the softer ground."

When Whittaker arrived at the ground the heavens opened. The rain hadn't deterred a good number of spectators however, who were already there waiting for the gates to open.

By eleven o'clock the queues were lengthening and stretching back down Warwick Road towards the city centre. As the crowds thickened, the atmosphere built, with rattles and horns sounding in anticipation of the great event.

The Arsenal players had a light lunch at a quarter to mid-day and left for the ground an hour later.

By this time, Warwick Road was crammed with people; with the hubbub and excitement reaching fever pitch. Ellen Donnelly was a sixth form student at the High School on Lismore Place, adjacent to Warwick Road:

> Some friends and I were on a study period up in the library from where you could see out on to Warwick Road. We could see the thousands and thousands of people streaming down the road towards Brunton Park. It was an amazing sight.

Outside the ground, the rosette and programme sellers were doing a roaring trade. One of the programme sellers was Gerald Irwin, the clerk from the City Treasurer's who had gone to the original game on the Saturday, and been involved in the ticket sale at the Market Hall on the Tuesday. Although it was half day closing for shops and some businesses, it was a normal day for the Corporation workers, so Gerald had to get permission from his supervisor to attend the game and carry out his pre-match duties. Gerald recalls:

> Stanley Graham gave me permission to go but told me I had to be back at work afterwards to clear the afternoon mail. The atmosphere at the ground was great. I sold a thousand programmes. We were paid the princely some of 3s per hundred so I made three quid that game!

The schools were given a half day off so that those children (and presumably staff) lucky enough to get tickets could attend. It was later reported that the Headmaster of the High School wrote a letter of complaint to the football club saying it was disgusting that children should miss out on their education for a 'stupid' football match. (*Stupid? Get with the programme granddad.*)

After the ticket debacle of less than forty-eight hours earlier, all police leave was cancelled and one hundred and thirty of the local force were supplemented by one hundred and fifty men from the part-time territorial force. Two mounted officers on the obligatory white horses stood guard in the middle of the road outside the ground.

"*Programmes!*"

Among the thousands milling about outside were ticket touts (*no, it's not a new occurrence!*). 'Spivs' were trying to sell to ten times the face value of 1s 6d.

Enhanced security inside the ground...

...marshals the crowd

"ee, this is better than the bingo!"

Someone who didn't make the game was Ivor Broadis. Although a Sunderland player, Ivor was very much part of the Carlisle camp as he still lived in the city and trained with the squad during the week. A week earlier he had been struck low with sinusitis and was confined to bed – he therefore didn't see the original game or the replay.

His training colleagues' exploits the previous Saturday spread round the football world like wildfire however and representatives from Sunderland, Newcastle, Tottenham and Everton all travelled to Brunton Park in mischievous curiosity. The Wearside contingent included Len Shackleton and they visited their stricken teammate before going to Brunton Park. In the Directors' Box, there was no sign of any Prime Ministers, but the Mayor of Carlisle and the city's MP were present to see the next instalment of the David and Goliath adventure.

Down below in the dressing rooms, it is a hive of activity.

In the home dressing room skipper Alex McIntosh is propped up on a make-shift couch, receiving some intensive treatment from trainer Fred Ford. McIntosh has a thigh strain and the treatment includes electrical stimulation to the leg.

McIntosh is one of four players carrying injuries into the second biggest game of their careers. Yards away in the cramped room Ford's assistant Tommy McBain is treating Geoff Twentyman for a similar injury while Paddy Waters is waiting his turn to have the calf injury – sustained in the original game – attended to. Finally, Tommy Kinloch waits and wonders about his own muscle strain.

Centre-forward Jackie Lindsay has no chance of playing with his broken jaw, and Alec Scott and Bill Caton are still not fit, so Shankly has no option but to go with the same eleven who covered themselves in so much glory on Saturday.

The manager is going round his players talking them up and the opposition down, with his customary infectious energy and enthusiasm:

"I've just seen them gittin' off the bus – half of them are limpin', they can hardly walk.

"Joe Mercer's not even here – he's frightened of comin'. That Compton's playin' in his place – shouldda stuck to the cricket!

"Billy *san*, you've got that England full-back worried, show him who's boss again."

Not surprisingly, things are different in the Arsenal camp. Tom Whittaker has brought fourteen players to Carlisle and has the luxury of making a few changes. First choice goalkeeper George Swindon is still unavailable so Ted Platt will continue to deputise. One enforced change is that of the skipper Joe Mercer: he developed flu symptoms on Monday and has spent the week in bed (not that that stopped Shankly putting his interpretation on matter). Shankly was right – Mercer's place will be taken by Leslie Compton who had a slight muscle strain that kept him out of the first match, when he was replaced by Ray Daniel. But Daniel himself is dropped for the replay and Whittaker decides to completely re-shape his half-back line. The combative vice-captain Alex Forbes is moved from right-half to left-half, while his position is taken by the equally combative Arthur Shaw. Compton is briefed on Mercer's problems with Billy Hogan at Highbury and instructed to give Lionel Smith plenty of support when the Blues' winger gets the ball.

The final change that Whittaker makes is the most interesting of all. Ian MacPherson was born in Glasgow and played as a junior for Rangers. When war broke out he joined the RAF and became a Squadron Leader; such was his bravery and achievement that he was awarded two Distinguished Flying Crosses while flying Mosquitos as part of the Pathfinder Squadron. Interestingly, MacPherson took the place of Freddie Cox who himself was decorated with a DFC during the war.

If MacPherson wasn't quite unique in the Gunners' camp as far as war service was concerned, he certainly was as far as football service was; because in 1945 he actually guested for Carlisle United, playing a handful of games while stationed at Crosby in the last months of the war.

One of his best games came on Easter Monday, when he lined up alongside outstanding local players Bob Lawson, Joe 'hat-trick' Patrick and Spud Hayton, who spanned the gap between the war years and Shankly's tenure.

The game was a triumph for Carlisle in general and MacPherson in particular, who was at the heart of most of United's good work in a 6–1 drubbing of a Forces Select XI.

The Scot was a languid winger and was signed by Arsenal from Notts County just after the war. He had an inauspicious start to his Arsenal career, playing in their first post war League fixture that saw them hammered 6–1 by Wolves. He and the team redeemed themselves however, by winning the League Title in 1948. MacPherson would go on to play over 150 games for the club but remained an enigmatic figure, drifting in and out of the first team, and – according to his manager Tom Whittaker – drifting in and out of games. Whittaker wrote of MacPherson in his autobiography:

> He was an exasperating player. He could be brilliant, at times almost better than Matthews. Yet at others he could be so ineffective that fans would pull out handfuls of hair while watching him.

MacPherson will now play his first game at Brunton Park for six years. The chairman of United John Corrieri, has done his best to provide facilities to which his auspicious guests are accustomed. The short walk from the players' changing facilities has been lined with carpet and potted flowers. With no covered tunnel, the players will be among the crowd within seconds of leaving their dressing room.

Finally, by 1:50pm all the treatment has been administered, all of the instructions have been issued. It's time.

A gate of 21,215 is in a frenzy of excitement. Young Paul Daley is in the Warwick Road End straining on tiptoes to see the arrival of the players.

John Peel and the hounds walk out on to the field

A cacophony of noise greets first the hounds, as they are walked to the centre circle, followed by Twinkletoes and Olga; the ear-splitting roar is then cranked up to maximum volume as Alex McIntosh leads the Blues out.

Finally, between the dark-clothed and flat-capped spectators in the Paddock, flashes of bright red and white can be seen: the Arsenal players are picking their way through the crowd and on to the field. The players who in an eighteen month period have walked out on to the Maracana in Rio and at Wembley, now walk out on to Brunton Park, Carlisle. After the usual few minutes of players dashing back and forth to warm up, the referee Mr Rogers calls the two skippers forward. McIntosh shakes hands with Alex Forbes, in Joe Mercer's absence. It's Carlisle's Alex who calls correctly as he did on Saturday. He decides to kick towards the Waterworks End and invites the visitors to kick-off. With a shrill of Rogers's whistle and a roar from the crowd, the game gets underway.

With the confidence gained from the first game, Carlisle start without any inhibition. After three minutes Billy Hogan gets his first touch after a couple of passes are exchanged between Jimmy Jackson and Phil Turner. The noise level increases as the crowd – half of whom witnessed his display in person; half of whom watched it at the Lonsdale Cinema – anticipate more wizardry from the wing man. He is immediately faced by his adversary Lionel Smith but this time Alex Forbes is in close attendance; Hogan enters a footrace with the full-back towards the by line and the ball ricochets between the two. Both glance earnestly towards the Mr Rogers and much to Smith's relief, the decision is a goal-kick to Arsenal.

Both teams soon settle into a quick, passing game that defies the poor surface – one reporter describes it as 'gluey'. Logie and MacPherson combine with a neat interchange on the Arsenal right, but Logie's final thrust is checked by an alert Geoff Twentyman; he plays the ball in one movement to Jackson who plays a first time ball to Jack Billingham but the centre-forward loses control and the ball runs through to Platt.

Both attacking units are easy on the eye with their slick passing and moving until it gets to the final third where Twentyman of Carlisle and Forbes of Arsenal marshal their respective defences to clear the danger.

It's difficult in these early stages to distinguish between the abilities of the two sides and therefore improbable to believe that there are two divisions between them.

The visitors then threaten twice in a minute but Twentyman thwarts centre-forward Peter Goring on both occasions. The ball then breaks to MacPherson on the Arsenal right and his loping, swaying run takes him into the box where there is a coming together with left-back Norman Coupe; the Arsenal player appeals for a penalty but Rogers waves play on. For all of the good play from each team, it is nine minutes before the first decent effort on goal, and it comes from the home side.

Inevitably it is Billy Hogan who is the architect: his quick interchange with Phil Turner ends with the latter sending in a snap-shot that the 'keeper Platt manages to first block and then – to the 'ooos' of the crowd – smothers it at the second attempt.

With Billy becoming more prominent, attention from the opposition is increased and the crowd give howls of derision as Don Roper brings him down in midfield. After fifteen minutes of the replay, there is little doubt that the minnows are giving the Cup Holders plenty to think about – but Arsenal are about to get a little respite.

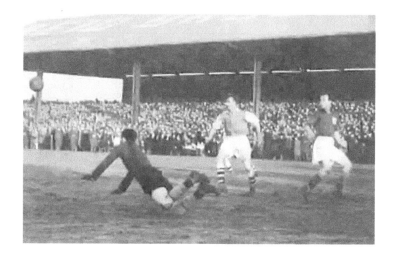

Jim MacLaren with a flying interception in the first half

Ex-Blue Ian MacPherson goes close

The free kick is cleared and Logie combines with MacPherson again but fellow Scot MacLaren just gets enough on the ball to divert it for a corner, with seventeen minutes on the clock. From the resultant kick it is none other than Billy Hogan, this time in defensive mode, who clears the Carlisle lines. The ball is on half way and instantly Leslie Compton plays a short pass to Forbes who moves it quickly forward to the playmaker Logie. Centre-forward Peter Goring has drifted out to the left wing and receives the ball almost at the corner flag; he looks up and sends in a cross with his left foot.

It is always said that centre-forwards are among the best crossers of a ball, as they always know exactly where it needs to be delivered to; such is the case here. To date, keeper Jimmy MacLaren hasn't had a meaning-ful touch of the ball and thankfully there has been no need to repeat his heroics of six days ago. As Goring's cross comes over however, he makes a catastrophic error of judgement: he leaves his line to intercept the cross but

– as one reporter observed – appears to catch his studs in the heavy goal-mouth. The upshot is that MacLaren loses the flight of the ball and it drifts over his head. It's too much to hope that Arsenal would be so negligent in their attacking play and, sure enough, there is Goring's striking partner Reg Lewis to head unopposed into the gaping net.

Reg Lewis scores Arsenal's first goal

Paul Daley is standing behind the goal at the Warwick Road End and sees Lewis's goal. ("We all thought that was it – they'll hammer us now," he remembers.)

But far from deflating the Carlisle players, the opening goal of the tie appear appears to ignite the home side, as blue waves start to attack the Waterworks End of the ground. The combative Waters is complemented by the deft touches of Jimmy Jackson in midfield; the crowd are impressed by Tommy Kinloch's efforts to win the ball but then his poor distribution undoes his hard work, much to their frustration.

Out wide meanwhile, McCue on the left, and Hogan – combining well with Turner – on the right, are causing their international opposition to scramble in defence. Jack Billingham is also doing his best to cause problems for the centre of the Arsenal defence. The period of play was highlighted by the reporter from the *Carlisle Journal*:

> Then came one of the finest attacking spells I have ever seen Carlisle produce. Undismayed by the fact that luck had turned its back on them they swept up-field on the attack and the Arsenal defence went through a gruelling spell. It seemed inevitable that Carlisle must score sooner or later.

Increasingly Hogan and Turner are taking charge, giving Lionel Smith more problems; left-half Alex Forbes is continually shuttling across to snuff out the danger. But with Waters, Kinloch and Jackson harrying away in midfield the ball keeps coming back.

If Smith gets the odd breather, it simply means that his defensive colleagues Walley Barnes and Arthur Shaw on the right are getting a similar time from Alex McCue. After twenty five minutes it's United's left-winger who ghosts in and head towards goal; Platt keeps it out but the rebound goes back to McCue who snatches at his shot and it goes wide.

Logie and MacPherson on the Arsenal right give their defensive colleagues a little respite with a neat juggling interchange that leads to centre-forward Goring beating MacLaren to the cross, but there is Norman Coupe on the line – as he was in a similar incident at Highbury – to keep the score at a deficit of one.

After half an hour, it seems absurd to suggest there are two divisions between the two teams, such is United's influence on the game – every man is playing his part. They come again with Hogan just shooting wide; moments later Hogan again sets up McCue who forces Platt to turn it over for a corner. The resultant corner is one of the few times the home side wastes possession – it's taken short to Waters who also goes short to McCue but the winger slips on the wet surface and the ball runs into touch.

On thirty-seven minutes Carlisle finally get their reward: inevitably it is Billy Hogan who starts a move half way inside the Arsenal half; he skips this way and that with his low centre of gravity and steals half a yard on Smith. The winger quickens the play with a short pass infield to Phil Turner who times his run perfectly through the inside-right channel; Turner's darting runs has the Arsenal defence in panic and he cracks in a shot on the run that Platt can only parry – there is McCue supporting from the left to slam the ball into the net. The ground erupts.

Alex McCue slams in the equaliser

This really is on!

(Willie Cannon was a young man standing in the Scratching Pen and remembers the roar today, "When we equalised it was great – I thought the roof was going to come off!")

The Arsenal machine is now spluttering and misfiring; Leslie Compton misses his kick completely and Platt has to scramble from his goal to just about beat Billingham to the loose ball.

The one down side for Carlisle is that some of the players are showing signs of the injuries they are carrying on the heavy surface. Most noticeably is the lionhearted Waters who goes down again and has to receive treatment from the trainer Fred Ford. Ford administers the wet sponge to the troublesome muscle and tells Waters to hang on for another five minutes when he will give him some more treatment at half-time.

Two minutes before the break comes a pivotal moment of the match, and the second seminal moment of the whole tie. Kinloch and Jackson combine in midfield to feed the maestro Hogan who slips Smith for the umpteenth time. Billy fires an angle cross shot that flies past Ted Platt at full-stretch; behind the keeper is right-back Walley Barnes and in an act of desperation he mirrors Platt's dive, with greater success: he reaches for the ball and fists around the post. Remarkably, referee Rogers fails to see the blatant hand-ball, and gives a goal-kick, seemingly believing that the ball hit the post and went wide. The mild mannered Hogan later recalled his incredulity:

> Barnes admitted punching the ball away afterwards. I think it was the only time [in my career] that I spoke to the referee on the field because the handling was so obvious.

The original hand of God – Walley Barnes at Brunton Park in 1951

Hogan's fury is echoed by the home fans who are incensed by the decision. Rogers blows for half-time but instead of basking in the greatest twenty minutes any Carlisle side had played in their modest history, the fans are genuinely angry that there team aren't in front. The outstanding period has surpassed the team's achievements on Saturday. The unanimous opinion in the press box is that Carlisle deserves to be in front.

Down below in the Carlisle changing room there is a feeling of belonging at this level. Bill Shankly is buzzing round his players telling them that they are outplaying the Cup Holders – for once, this is not a case of the famous Shankly-psychology. "Ye can be legends this day!" he continually tells his men.

The one question is can the would-be legends keep this pace up for another 45 minutes, especially with some of them carrying heavy knocks – most notably Paddy Waters. He is receiving intensive treatment as Shankly blasts out the instructions for the second half; Waters's muscle injury is getting worse now that he is at rest.

The players come out for the second half and the noise level rises: this is already the greatest day in Brunton Park's history, now there is a chance of a result that will never be surpassed, whatever the club achieves in the future.

The cracking pace at which the game has been played in the first half is again in evidence. The break appears to have done the visitors a power of good as they seem to have regained the composure they showed in the first quarter of the game. They win an early corner that is cleared and when the ball is played back in, Jimmy Logie is signalled offside as he shapes to regain the lead for his team.

Jim MacLaren shovels away an effort in the second half as Norman Coupe covers on the line

At the other end, Compton, Shaw and Forbes are quickly closing down the United attackers, but that doesn't prevent the goal-scoring hero Alex McCue firing in a cross shot that goes narrowly wide. Moments later United win it back and Turner goes on a weaving run before playing in centre-forward Jack Billingham but the he shoots weakly and Platt gathers.

Paul Daley stares on in wide-eyed wonderment at his heroes who are now attacking their favoured Warwick Road End and threatening to take the lead. (Paul swears today, "If Jackie Lindsay was playing, we would have won.")

Then, five minutes into the second half, Arsenal forge their first meaningful attack for twenty five minutes; it is snuffed out by the skipper McIntosh at the expense of a corner.

The goalmouth at the Waterworks End is a jostling mass of red, white and blue. MacPherson sends over the corner and a melee ensues with Twentyman hacking it away only for it to hit Lewis on the back; goalkeeper MacLaren dives bravely at the leather ball that is becoming a bit of a dead weight in the heavy goalmouth but it squirts out of his reach as players from both sides lunge towards it. Finally, more by accident than design, the ball finds its way to Jimmy Logie who is standing a yard from the near post. With MacLaren still on the ground and out of the game, the Arsenal playmaker manages to flick the ball with his studs before the full-backs can react on the line and it rolls gently across the white-wash and into the net.

From being denied a 2-1 lead at the same end a few minutes before the break, United now find themselves 2-1 down a few minutes after it.

The goal, however scrappy, acts as a settler for Arsenal who now look as though they will take control. Centre-half Leslie Compton is starting to move forward and bring his midfielders into play; Carlisle have to concede another corner. Over it comes and, with echoes of his heroics on Saturday, MacLaren rises high above the crowd; the ball comes back in but – like Logie earlier – Reg Lewis is flagged offside before he can make it three.

As the game moves towards the final quarter it is still in the balance. Despite the fact that they have conceded since the break, Carlisle are still mounting the odd attack, although they are becoming less frequent as the intensity shows no sign of abating. The next goal is everything – it is destined to be a personal tragedy for Jim MacLaren.

With twenty minutes to go Don Roper feeds Goring who has again drifted towards the Arsenal left. Goring crosses as he did in the first half and his ball is met by the perfectly positioned Reg Lewis; Lewis fails to make a decent connection however, and the ball bounces harmlessly towards the goalkeeper who is on his knees to field. Incredibly the slow moving ball seems to spin over the 'keeper's left arm and to his and the crowd's horror, dribbles over the line. Lewis – the man who scored both of Arsenal's goals in their last FA Cup tie, at Wembley – now has two at Brunton Park.

With the result now seemingly inevitable, Carlisle's attacks are becoming more infrequent, and the Arsenal defence is growing in stature. The visiting keeper Platt is becoming a spectator as his opposite number – despite his two howlers – is starting to work overtime as he did on Saturday to keep the score down. He gets away with a further misjudgement when he tears out of his goal to clear, only to be beaten to the ball by Lewis, who is now on a hat-trick, but his goal-bound effort is stopped by McIntosh.

The tide is now turning away from United but Billy Hogan has other ideas. Receiving the ball just inside the Arsenal half, he has his back to the ubiquitous Alex Forbes; with a drop of the shoulder and swift turn, Hogan appears to slip the shackles of Forbes but is immediately clattered by Goring who comes in from behind. The little man goes to the ground clutching the back of his leg; the Arsenal number six, Forbes, doesn't realise what has happened and moves to help Hogan up, Paddy Waters dashes across and piles in, pushing and shoving Forbes, who he believes has targeted the winger. The Irishman has to be restrained and the police and military quickly react to unrest amongst the spectators in the Paddock who have just witnessed the ugly scene a few yards in front of them.

The fractious atmosphere passes quickly as the wrongdoing appears to give Carlisle a new lease of life; they create two nice passing moves and again McCue goes close with another cross shot.

Back it goes to the other end with a thunderous shot from the unlikely source of right-half Arthur Shaw. His shot beats MacLaren but cannons against the bar and goes over.

But his team are to have the last word. With a few minutes remaining Logie and Roper combine, and after a slip by Tommy Kinloch, Goring finds himself clean through and makes no mistake in beating the onrushing MacLaren.

Peter Goring scores Arsenal's fourth

In a vain attempt to redress the unfair scoreline, United mount a final hurrah, but to no avail. Mr Rogers blows his whistle at 3:40pm and the great adventure is over.

As Jim MacLaren walks off the pitch, he is met by a reporter on the touchline who refers to Arsenal's first goal by asking, "What happened Jim?"

"I don't know," replies the 'keeper "I must have got stuck in the mud."

(MacLaren later told his daughter he regretted this little exchange as the following day the paper concerned printed the headline, 'Jim gets stuck in the mud!' "Never say anything to reporters," he advised his daughter after that experience.)

Thus, the Cup tie that had the city on tenterhooks for six days, came to a close. The Arsenal players were the first to congratulate their opponents; despite the scoreline, they knew how close they had come to an upset. They were quickly followed by their manager Tom Whittaker – he followed the Carlisle players into their dressing room and with Shankly's permission, addressed them:

> You gave me the biggest fright of my life. Don't give up on your fight for the Northern Section Championship. Go for it and make certain of it. You have got it in your pocket so make sure of it.

In the United boardroom, pressmen and League club representatives were full of praise for the wonderful performance from the boys in blue. The consensus was that Arsenal were fitter and just about deserved the victory, but the 4–1 scoreline in no way reflected the tie. As one reporter summarised:

> Arsenal were a stronger and better team than they were at Highbury. The team changes made an improvement. Compton's reappearance at centre-half especially. This stalwart half-back is certainly a great defender, and a fine distributer of play particularly with his head.

> Carlisle can hold their heads high however. They went out of the cup in the knowledge that Arsenal were not three goals better than themselves. They held the might of Arsenal for fifty minutes. Even when the visitors got their second goal there was always the chance that Carlisle could still pull it off. But it was the third Arsenal goal that sealed the fate of Carlisle. It can be said for MacLaren that he more than anybody else brought this replay to Brunton Park and in the course of it, though beaten rather softly, he did make several superlative saves from Arsenal efforts that really deserved to score.

Not a man spared himself, nor shirked a single tackle. It was a great fighting display on both occasions by a lighter team whose skill indeed was emphasised by their physical disparity.

The final word inevitably went to Shankly. In his post-match interview he was as generous as Whittaker in front of the press:

> Nobody can dispute that we put up a wonderful show in both matches. The team that beat us is one of the most formidable in the game and have been for twenty years.

Back in the dressing room, he was as defiant as ever:

> Boys, ye've just lost tae the greatest side in England – but it took them two games tae beat us!

Postscript

The great adventure (for Carlisle that is) was over. Strangely, the tie seemed to almost destabilize both clubs' seasons. Arsenal sneaked through the next round against Northampton but then lost to Manchester United in the fifth round. They also slipped from the top of the League and finished a relatively modest fifth. They would soon be back however, reaching the Cup Final again in 1952 and winning their seventh League Championship in 1953.

(Joe Mercer became England [caretaker] manager in the early 1970s. After one game, local journalist Ross Brewster managed to grab a quick word with him and asked him if he remembered the game. Even at a distance of twenty plus years and season after season of success as a player and a manager, Mercer instantly replied, "Yes, I'll never forget it. I was run ragged by a little bandy legged chap they had on the wing!")

Carlisle United of course were operating in a completely different world from Arsenal and following the tie Shankly sought to re-focus the minds on their 1951 promotion push.

Once the draw for the big game was made he feared the tie would undermine the solid League campaign. Strangely that didn't happen *before* the game was played, but there is evidence to suggest it did *afterwards*. Shankly himself even seemed a little unsettled by the Arsenal replay; despite his generous assessment of his opponents immediately after the game, he was less magnanimous when asked to reflect on the game by a local journalist in the days following:

It was a great shame they felt the need to kick Billy Hogan into the terracing. I felt we could have given them a good game up here. It's done now, we have all shook hands. Billy is naturally disappointed, as he knows he had the beating of their England full-back. It's a tough lesson but we have all learned from it. Billy has taken a nasty knock to his knee, it looks very painful and he may be out of the team for some time. I'm very disappointed, not at losing but at the way Arsenal resorted to acts of thuggery.

The mild-mannered Hogan himself concurred with his manager, when he reflected on the game years later in an interview with United historian Paul Harrison. He sounded unusually bitter about the experience:

The Arsenal team that came to us in the replay had a separate mentality to the one we noticed in London five days earlier. This time they meant business. I was a marked man. Each time I got the ball one and sometimes two Arsenal players clattered into me. It wasn't fun at all. I asked the referee for a bit of support but he would just tell me to shut and up get on with the game. It wasn't as if I was deliberately throwing myself to the ground on each challenge. I was getting kicked up in the air.

All I remember is taking on the left-back and seeing three players haring at me. It bloody hurt I tell you. I thought I had broken something, I don't think Muhammad Ali could have hurt me more than those Arsenal players did. I knew I wasn't going to be able to continue; my right leg was painful and both pins were covered in bruises. Mighty Arsenal? More like mighty cheats that day. They really worked us over. They didn't win because of football skill; they won because they were tougher and harder. After the game their manager came up to me and apologised for the treatment I suffered. He told me that sometimes football skills cannot be matched, so you must do what you feel right to contain the threat. In my case it was kicking me, nothing like sporting behaviour.

A week after the game, Geoff Twentyman was called up for his national service; a week after that, Carlisle's 15-match unbeaten league run came to an end. Wrexham inflicted a 0–2 home defeat on the Blues – their first home League defeat in twelve months.

With the centre-half's temporary departure, the solidity of the of Waters, Twentyman and Kinloch combination was upset and Geoff Hill, Dennis Stokoe and Jack Billingham would all be called upon to fill in at various points with mixed results.

Momentum was regained somewhat with a five match winning streak in February but more disappointment was to follow for the fans a month later when the club sold both Jackie Lindsay and Jack Billingham to Southport on the same day.

They were replaced in the squad by Jimmy Johnson from Grimsby but the disruption to the squad resulted in a fairly regular win-loss-draw sequence that resulted in them coming up short of their stated intention: they finished third behind Rotherham and Mansfield. (The goalless draw at home to Rotherham on Good Friday attracted a crowd of 20,454 – a new League record crowd.)

To make matters worse for Carlisle fans, the ambitious Bill Shankly took his next step towards managerial immortality by moving to Second Division Grimsby Town, who had courted him throughout the season. He explained his thought process in his autobiography:

> …all of them [the board of directors] were devoutly loyal to the club, including my uncle. The problem was that I could stand no more financial restrictions placed upon me, the buying of more experience and better players never came into the equation. If I had wanted someone, somebody better than I had, then I would have to sell three, maybe four players to raise the cash. It was a never-ending circle. I really enjoyed my time at the club and love the area, Carlisle is a smashing city it will always hold a very special place in my heart.

Although his time at Brunton Park was brief, analysis of his record stands favourable scrutiny.

Managerial Record:
League Matches: 95
Won: 42
Drawn: 31
Lost: 22

1948–49: 15th in Division Three North
1949–50: 9th in Division Three North
1950–51: 3rd in Division Three North

The players he left behind enjoyed mixed success during the remainder of their careers. One player he didn't leave behind was goal-scoring winger Alex McCue: the Scot followed his manager to Grimsby after only 32 games (and 11 goals) in the blue shirt. The move suited all parties as it meant that Carlisle never did have to pay Falkirk a transfer fee for the winger!

McCue's opposite wingman Billy Hogan was surely capable of playing a much higher level but chose to stay with Carlisle. In September 1952 he suffered a terrible knee injury after an appalling challenge in a match against Crewe. He only played another thirty seven games between then and April 1956 when he played his last game for the club. He never lost his love for the game however and after retiring back home to Salford, he continued to play in the local Manchester leagues until he was 62! He eventually retired to Cornwall.

Of the local lads, Norman Coupe and Spud Hayton were sold to Rochdale for £500 each as part of a deal that brought another [future] great, Jimmy Whitehouse, to the club.

At the end of *his* career, skipper Alex McIntosh became a bookmaker and then a licensee, while fellows Scots Tommy Kinloch and Jimmy Jackson eventually returned to Glasgow.

Paddy Waters bought a newsagent's business and remained in the city for the rest of his life.

The two other players who never actually lived in Carlisle (along with Billy Hogan), Phil Turner and Jack Billingham, moved back to the areas familiar to them in early life: Turner to Rhyl and Billingham to his native West Midlands.

Shankly never had favourites as far as players were concerned – he believed strongly in giving everyone a fair chance. But he did develop close friendships with players and staff throughout his career that would last well into retirement. One such friendship was with Blues' centre-forward Jackie Lindsay.

Although Lindsay pre-dated Shankly's reign as Carlisle manager, he shared all the qualities of hard work, strong principles and fierce loyalty. When it is considered that both of them came from Ayrshire it is no surprise that they got on so well together. An example of their friendship came most Thursday afternoons during Shankly's tenure.

The manager used to live at Tullie Street just a few hundred yards from Brunton Park in one direction, and a few hundred yards from Melbourne Park – where there were several football pitches – in the other. As Thursday was half day closing in Carlisle in those days, there was a Thursday afternoon league for local teams. The bad news for Bill is that Thursday was also wash-day in the Shankly household, which meant that the football manager 'had to give way' to the dutiful husband and help wife Ness with the washing. (Ness shared Shankly's can-do attitude by regularly washing the players' kit!)

To combat this Shankly would prime Lindsay beforehand, telling him to come round to the house on the pretext of asking Ness if Bill could come over to Melbourne Park to see a particular player Jackie had his eye on. Apparently it caused many a ruck between Mr and Mrs Shankly but the upshot usually was that poor Ness had to stay home and do all the washing, while the two Hectors went over the road *tae watch some fitba'*.

Jackie Lindsay returned to Carlisle for a brief playing spell in 1954. In the three intervening years he played with Southport and Wigan, where he wrote two other noteworthy chapters in the Lindsay legend. In February 1952 when playing for Southport, he scored a hat-trick in three minutes, equalling a League record (the feat sadly didn't gain much national coverage as it was the same day on which King George VI died!).

The other highlight came when playing for non-League Wigan in the third round of the FA Cup in 1954. Lindsay had missed out on Carlisle's big Cup tie three years earlier, but in what was almost a mirror image of the Carlisle/Arsenal tie, Wigan were drawn away at Newcastle United.

Incredibly the non-Leaguers achieved a 2–2 draw at the Tyneside giants and – like Carlisle – gave as good as they got for long spells in the replay before Newcastle ran out 3–2 winners. By coincidence, playing opposite Lindsay in the black and white stripes was Ivor Broadis, the man who signed him for Carlisle in 1947. (Broadis was at the height of his playing career and scored in both games against Wigan. He went on to represent England at the World Cup later that summer.)

Jackie Lindsay returned to his adopted 'home' for a brief spell and remained in Carlisle following his retirement a year later. The Scot remained close friends with Bill Shankly for the rest of his life. Lindsay's son John remembers:

> Shankly came to our house many a time. He never had anything to eat and just drank Brazilian tea. He would sit with my dad for hours talking about tactics and acting out scenarios on the coffee table with matchsticks for players. And when he wasn't in the area, the two would be on the phone for hours talking about the game. I know he told my dad once that his biggest regret was never getting the chance to manage Scotland. They were really good pals – I think it was a Scottish thing.

The one player from Shankly's squad to make the big time was almost inevitably Geoff Twentyman. In 1953 Wolves placed a £10k bid in for the centre-half who wanted to pair the youngster with their own emerging talent, Billy Wright. (Had the move gone through Twentyman may well have been part of the great Wolves side of the late '50s that appeared in the inaugural European Cup.) Instead he moved to Liverpool in a £12,000 deal that came just at the right time for Carlisle who used the money to build a new stand following a fire at Brunton Park!

Bill Shankly arrived as manager of Liverpool in 1959, just as Twentyman ended his high-level playing career. He moved to Northern Ireland to take up the role of player-manager of Ballymena, where he won their first Ulster Cup in 1961. Twentyman returned briefly to Carlisle in 1963 as Alan Ashman's first signing before becoming Hartlepools' manager in the summer of 1965.

He may never have distinguished himself as a manager, but Geoff Twentyman's place in British football is assured through his work as a player-spotter. Bill Shankly took him back to Liverpool as chief scout in 1967 and history beckoned. All football supporters know about Shankly, Paisley, Fagan et al; but what many don't realise is that it was Geoff Twentyman who scouted and signed all the great players who would dominate the English game for the next two decades.

Twentyman and Shankly remained friends throughout their lives, due mainly to their values and footballing philosophy. Both believed players with a northern (or Scottish) soul had a greater desire and affiliation to a northern club. With this in mind, Twentyman developed a network of scouts throughout Lancashire and Yorkshire. Further north, one of his scouts was Jazza Boyle who, in adulthood, became active in the local game. Twentyman would travel to Carlisle from his Merseyside home, stay at Jazza's house and the two would then travel up to Scotland the following day looking at players.

Jazza remembers the time when Geoff took him to Liverpool for the first time to meet Shankly:

> The three of us were in Shankly's office and Geoff introduced me as one of his new scouts. We got to talking about the famous '51 tie and Shankly asked if I was there. I told him that I was at the replay but I couldn't afford to go to the original game. Shankly snapped, "You were a young boy *san*, you could've walked!"

Twentyman may not have distinguished himself as a manager but there was a player in the Carlisle squad of 1950 did.

George Dick wrote training manuals and became one of the first qualified FA coaches. He promptly moved abroad and took up the manager's job at Racing Club Ghent in Belgium. He moved to Denmark as the chief of Boldkluben 1909 (in Odense) in 1957, before having a season managing Turkish giants Galatasaray. He then went back to Odense and led 1909 to their first Danish Championship in 1959–60. (Tragically George died in a car accident a few months later).

The other managerial success story from the Carlisle group came in the figure of trainer Fred Ford. He had begun his coaching career at Brunton Park and progressed to national status with the England B team and the under-23 side. In 1955 he moved to Bristol Rovers, gaining widespread recognition as their first team coach. His first managerial job came across the city in 1960. He moved from Bristol to Swindon in 1969 and led the Robins to victory in the Anglo Italian League Cup (1969) and the Anglo Italian Cup (1970).

Two other United players of the period stayed in the game but in another capacity. Following his outstanding playing career, Ivor Broadis became a journalist, covering games in his adopted home city of Carlisle, as well as reporting on the three big North East clubs.

Similarly, at the end of *his* playing career, Dennis Stokoe took off his boots and picked up the journalist's pad and pen to write for papers in Manchester and the North East. (Dennis gradually broadened his journalistic horizons and became chief business reporter with the *Newcastle Journal* in 1969.)

And the young supporters who followed their team to Highbury on that winter's day in 1951; who stood in the queue for tickets; or who just revelled in the general excitement? Well, they grew into adulthood, became parents and grandparents, travelled the world and experienced their own triumphs and tragedies, and gradually locked the Arsenal adventure away, along with a thousand other fond, distant memories. That was until some inquisitive local writer sought them out to ask about their experiences half a lifetime ago.

The adventure they experienced served as a welcome distraction to them and their contemporaries. Everyone interviewed remembers the times with some fondness but invariably recalls the hardship endured by them and their families.

Nationally, Clement Atlee's Labour Party had scraped home in the 'cost of living' election of 1950 (by five seats), but it was clear there was no magic wand solution to the country's ills. With rationing still in operation, and the war in Korea having a disastrous effect on the country's fragile economy, housewives were facing more difficult shopping conditions *after* the [world] war than *during* it.

Another election was called less than a year later and the electorate had to listen to the negative campaigning of both major parties: the Conservatives emphasising the austerity and government bureaucracy, while Labour accused their opponents of warmongering and continually reminded the electorate of the Tories' record on unemployment.

When it came to crunch day (25 October 1951), with the Government's foreign and domestic policies seemingly faltering, it was 'the old toss pot' himself who was returned to power. Despite leading the country through the war years, Winston's triumph in 1951 was actually his first General Election victory.

But even the Tories' triumph was hardly a resounding mandate for change – a swing of one per cent gave Churchill the keys to Number 10 by just twenty-six seats. (Another interesting consideration of the period is that despite the electorate being so disillusioned, the turn-out was tremendous. The Labour Party polled nearly 14 million votes, the record number of votes recorded by any British political party in any election to that time, but still lost!)

Hardship continued until 1954 when restrictions on the sale and purchase of meat and bacon were lifted; rationing had finally ended in its entirety, a full fourteen years after it was implemented. (The sting in the tail for the consumer was that prices initially soared as demand far outstripped supply.)

Back at Brunton Park meanwhile, following Shankly's departure, the small Third Division club came under the tenure of Fred Emery and Ivor Powell before Alan Ashman led the club to that illusive promotion to the second tier of the League and on to what would prove to be the most successful period in the club's history.

The source of all the excitement related in this volume, the FA Cup, continues today, but it has long since lost much of its magic. In the days covered here, the Cup was as big as the League Championship; nowadays it is viewed by most of the big clubs as being an almost inconvenient distraction from the riches of European football.

It does however still throw up the odd romantic story. For example, in an unbelievable coincidence, Arsenal and Carlisle met again at the same stage of the competition, exactly fifty years later to the day on 6 January 2001. (That's where the romance began and ended however. No books will ever be written about this largely dull encounter that saw Arsenal go through the motions to achieve a 1–0 victory.)

And the city that lost itself to the romance of the cup all those years ago changed as well, of course. Its great employers who enjoyed so much success, and whose paternalistic approach to their employees developed such a great sense of community in the process, enjoyed mixed fortunes in the latter half of the twentieth century.

Hudson Scott remained a large employer but eventually lost its name and simply became 'The Metal Box'. Similarly Carr's Biscuits continued on the same site before being taken over in 1972. The difference between the two is that the Carr's name lived (and still lives) on, despite the factory eventually becoming part of a multi-national organisation.

Cowans and Sheldon meanwhile would gradually disappear altogether. They would first become associated with various other giants of their particular industry, which in turn would lead to mergers, acquisitions and takeovers over the following decades before the giant yard in Carlisle disappeared completely before the end of the century.

As for W.B. Anderson's – it continued to operate from its warehouse on West Walls before moving up to Durranhill in 1959. The building on West Walls however – known as 'The Smiddy' because it was a Blacksmith's Shop in the nineteenth century – was so popular with customers it remained, with Claude Daley running it on his own until his retirement in 1970. The company was sold to West Cumberland Farmers six years later.

But the last word of all should go to the man who made everyone believe that miracles could happen. Bill Shankly left his first managerial job in Carlisle and went on to become a legend in the profession and someone who was adored by millions. Perhaps such adoration was because his mantra remained the same; wherever he went and whatever he achieved, his view remained steadfast: "The people who matter the most are the ones that come through the turnstiles. A manager has got to identify himself with the people."

PRINCIPLE SOURCES

Books

Barnes, Walley, *Captain of Wales*, GCR Books Ltd, 2012

Darby, Tom, *Talking Shankly*, Mainstream Publishing Company (Edinburgh) Ltd, 2001

Cowing, Ronald; Lawson, Martin; Willcox, Bill, *The Carlisle United Story*, Lakeland Publications, 1974

Harrison, Paul, *Carlisle's Cult Heroes,* Know the Score Books, 2007

Harrison, Paul, *Carlisle United The Complete Record*, Breedon Books, 2008

Hughes, Simon, *Geoff Twentyman – Secret Diary of a Liverpool Scout,* Sport Media, 2011

James, Gary, *Joe Mercer – Football with a Smile,* ACL & Polar Publishing, 1994

Shankly, Bill, *My Story*, Sport Media, 2011

Soar, Phil & Tyler, Martin, *Arsenal 1886–1986 – The Official Centenary History of Arsenal Football Club*, Book Club Associates, 1986

Whittaker, Tom, *Tom Whittaker's Arsenal Story*, Sporting Handbooks Ltd, 1957

Wild, KA, *Carlisle United, Fifty Seasons On,* 1985

Printed Papers

Arsenal programmes

Files of the *Carlisle Journal*

Files of the *Cumberland News*

Files of the *Evening News*

Files of the *Evening News & Star*

Websites

www.arsenal.com

www.carlisleunited.co.uk

www.neilbrown.newcastlefans.com/carlisle/carlisle

www.newsandstar.co.uk

www.soccerbase.com

www.statto.com

www.thebeautifulhistory.wordpress.com

www.wikipedia.com

ND - #0282 - 270225 - C0 - 234/156/13 - PB - 9781780913674 - Gloss Lamination